South America

phrase book & dictionary

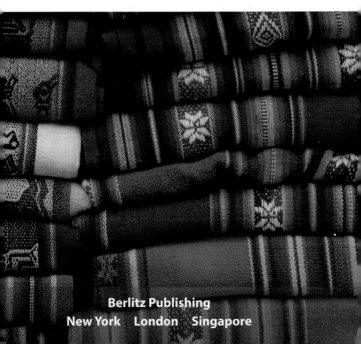

Berlitz Publishing
New York   London   Singapore

Contacting the Editors
Every effort has been made to provide accurate information in this publication, but changes are inevitable. The publisher cannot be responsible for any resulting loss, inconvenience or injury. We would appreciate it if readers would call our attention to any errors or outdated information. We also welcome your suggestions; if you come across a relevant expression not in our phrase book, please contact us at: **comments@berlitzpublishing.com**

All Rights Reserved
© 2015 Berlitz Publishing/APA Publications (UK) Ltd.
Berlitz Trademark Reg. U.S. Patent Office and other countries. Marca Registrada. Used under license from Berlitz Investment Corporation.

First Printing: 2015
Printed in China

Senior Commissioning Editor: Kate Drynan
Translation: updated by Alingua/Wordbank
Simplified phonetics: updated by Wordbank
Cover & Interior Design: Beverley Speight
Production update: A M Services
Production Manager: Vicky Mullins
Picture Researcher: Beverley Speight
Cover Photos: All Yadid Levy except coins Abe Nowitz; Yellow wall San Miguel Allende

Interior Photos: Yadid Levy 6-44; Anna Mockford & NIck Bonetti 66-107, 128, 144, 162; Abe Nowitz 124, 127, 131-138, 147, 149, 155, 159, 161, 164, 188-193, 198, 212; Beverley Speigh 143, 158, 207, 215-217; Corrie Wingate 139, 148, 165, 195, 199-206, 209, 214; Alex Havret 140, 151, 152, 156; 167 Britta Jaschinski 167, 170; iStockphoto 166, 168

Contents

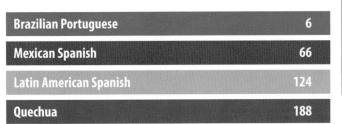

How to use this Book

> Sometimes you see two alternatives separated by a slash. Choose the one that's right for your situation.

ESSENTIAL

Where's the pharmacy [chemist]?
Onde fica a farmácia? *aund fee·kuh uh fuhr·mah·see·uh*

What time does the pharmacy open/close?
A que horas abre/fecha a farmácia? *uh keh aw·ruhz ah·breh/feh·shuh uh fuhr·mah·see·uh*

What would you recommend for...?
O que é que me recomenda para...? *oo keh eh keh meh reh·koo·mehn·duh puh·ruh...*

> Words you may see are shown in YOU MAY SEE boxes.

YOU MAY SEE...

CHEGADAS — arrivals
PARTIDAS — departures
ENTREGA DE BAGAGEM — baggage claim

> Any of the words or phrases listed can be plugged into the sentence below.

At the Hotel

When's...
A que horas é... para...? *uh kee aw·ruhz eh... puh·ruh*

the (first) bus to
o (primeiro) ónibus *uh (pree·may·roo) aw·nee·boo*

the (next) flight
o (próximo) vôo *oo (praw·see·moo) vau·oo*

the (last) train
o (último) trem *oo (ool·tee·moo) treng*

Brazilian Portuguese phrases appear in purple.

Read the simplified pronunciation as if it were English.

Relationships

Hello.   **Oi.** *au·hee*
How are you?   **Tudo bem?** *Too·duh beng*
Fine, thanks.   **Bem, obrigado m/obrigada f.** *behm
                                aw·bree·gah·doo/aw·bree·gah·duh*

Excuse me!   **Desculpe!** *dehz·kool·peh*
For Numbers, see page 8.

Related phrases can be found by going to the page number indicated.

When different gender forms apply, the masculine form is followed by *m*; feminine by *f*

Parking can be difficult in big cities. Always lock your car and never leave anything in sight (even if you consider it not valuable) as it can encourage break-ins.

Information boxes contain relevant country, culture and language tips.

Expressions you may hear are shown in You May Hear boxes.

YOU MAY HEAR...

O que deseja? *oo keh deh·zeh·zsuh*   What would you like?
Recomendo... *reh·koo·mehn·doo...*   I recommend...
Bom apetite. *bohng uh·peh·tee·teh*   Enjoy your meal.

Color-coded side bars identify each section of the book.

Brazilian Portuguese

Essentials

Hello.	**Oi.** _au·hee_
Goodbye.	**Tchau.** _chah·oo_
Yes.	**Sim.** _seeng_
No.	**Não.** _nohm_
OK.	**O.K.** _aw·kay_
Excuse me!	**Desculpe!** _deh·skoolp_
Sorry!	**Perdão!** _pehr·dohm_
I'd like something…	**Queria algo…**
	keh·ree·uh ahl·goo…
How much/many?	**Quanto/Quantos?**
	kwuhn·too/kwuhn·toos
Where is the…?	**Onde está…?** _aund ee·stah…_
Please.	**Por favor.** _poor fuh·vaur_
Thank you.	**Obrigado** _m_/**Obrigada** _f._
	aw·bree·gah·doo/aw·bree·gah·duh
You're welcome.	**De nada.** _deh nah·duh_
Could you speak more slowly?	**Pode falar mais devagar?** _pawd fuh·lahr meyez deh·vuh·gahr_
Could you repeat that?	**Pode repetir?** _pawd reh·peh·teer_
I don't understand	**Não entendo.** _nohm ehn·tehn·doo_
Do you speak English?	**Fala inglês?** _fah·luh eng·lehz_
I don't speak (much) Portuguese.	**Não falo (muito) português.** _nohm fah·loo (mooee·too) poor·too·gehz_
Where are the restrooms [toilets]?	**Onde são os banheiros?** _aund sohm ooz bah·nyay·rooz_
Help!	**Socorro!** _soo·kau·rroo_

Numbers

0	**zero**	_zeh_•roo
1	**um _m_/uma _f_**	oong/_oo_•muh
2	**dois _m_/duas _f_**	doyz/_thoo_•uhz
3	**três**	trehz
4	**quatro**	_kwah_•troo
5	**cinco**	_seeng_•koo
6	**seis**	sayz
7	**sete**	seht
8	**oito**	_oy_•too
9	**nove**	nawv
10	**dez**	dehz
11	**onze**	aunz
12	**doze**	dauz
13	**treze**	trehz
14	**catorze**	kuh•_taurz_
15	**quinze**	keengz
16	**dezesseis**	dehz•eh•_sayz_
17	**dezessete**	dehz•eh•_seht_
18	**dezoito**	dehz•_oy_•too
19	**dezenove**	deh•zuh•_nawv_
20	**vinte**	veent

You'll find the pronunciation of the Brazilian Portuguese letters and words written in gray after each sentence to guide you. Simply pronounce these as if they were English, noting that any underlines and bolds indicate an additional emphasis or stress or a lengthening of a vowel sound. As you hear the language being spoken, you will quickly become accustomed to the local pronunciation and dialect.

21	**vinte e um** *m*/**uma** *f*	*veent ee oong/oo•muh*
22	**vinte e dois** *m*/**duas** *f*	*veent ee doyz/thoo•uhz*
30	**trinta**	*treeng•tuh*
31	**trinta e um** *m*/**uma** *f*	*treeng•tuh ee oong/oo•muh*
40	**quarenta**	*kwuh•rehn•tuh*
50	**cinquenta**	*seeng•kwehn•tuh*
60	**sessenta**	*seh•sehn•tuh*
70	**setenta**	*seh•tehn•tuh*
80	**oitenta**	*oy•tehn•tuh*
90	**noventa**	*noo•vehn•tuh*
100	**cem**	*sehn*
101	**cento e um** *m*/**uma** *f*	*sehn•too ee oong/oo•muh*
200	**duzentos** *m*/**duzentas** *f*	*doo•zehn•tooz/doo•zehn•tuhz*
500	**quinhentos** *m*/**quinhentas** *f*	*kee•nyehn•tooz/ kee•nyehn•tuhz*
1,000	**mil**	*meel*
10,000	**dez mil**	*dehz meel*
1,000,000	**um milhão**	*oong mee•lyohm*

Time

What time is it?	**Por favor, que horas são?** *poor fuh•vaur keh aw•ruhz sohm*
It's noon [midday].	**É meio-dia.** *eh may•oo dee•uh*
At midnight.	**À meia-noite.** *ah may•uh noyt*
From nine o'clock to five o'clock.	**Das nove às cinco horas.** *duhz nawv ahz seeng•koo aw•ruhz*
Twenty [after] past four.	**Quatro e vinte.** *kwah•troo ee veent*
A quarter to nine.	**Quinze para as nove.** *kinz puh•ruh uhz nawv*
5:30 a.m./p.m.	**Cinco e meia de manhã/da tarde.** *seeng•koo ee may•uh deh muh•nyuh/duh tahrd*

Days

Monday	**segunda-feira** *seh•goon•duh fay•ruh*
Tuesday	**terça-feira** *tehr•suh fay•ruh*
Wednesday	**quarta-feira** *kwahr•tuh fay•ruh*
Thursday	**quinta-feira** *keen•tuh fay•ruh*
Friday	**sexta-feira** *say•stuh fay•ruh*
Saturday	**sábado** *sah•buh•thoo*
Sunday	**domingo** *doo•meeng•goo*

Dates

yesterday	**ontem** _awn_·teng
today	**hoje** auzseh
tomorrow	**amanhã** uh·muh·_nuh_
day	**o dia** oo _dee_·uh
week	**a semana** uh seh·_muh_·nuh
month	**o mês** oo mehz
year	**o ano** oo _uh_·noo

Months

January	**Janeiro** zher·_nay_·roo
February	**Fevereiro** feh·_vray_·roo
March	**Março** _mahr_·soo
April	**Abril** uh·_breel_
May	**Maio** _meye_·oo
June	**Junho** _zsoo_·nyoo
July	**Julho** _zsoo_·lyoo
August	**Agosto** uh·_gaus_·too
September	**Setembro** seh·_tehm_·broo
October	**Outubro** aw·_too_·broo
November	**Novembro** noo·_vehm_·broo
December	**Dezembro** deh·_zehm_·broo

Arrival & Departure

I'm on vacation [holiday]/business.	**Estou de férias/em negócios.** *ee-stawoo deh feh-ree-uhz/eng neh-gaw-see-yooz*
I'm going to...	**Vou para...** *vawoo puh-ruh...*
I'm staying at the... Hotel.	**Estou no hotel...** *ee-stawoo noo aw-tehl...*

Money

Where's...?	**Onde é...?** *aund eh...*
the ATM	**o caixa eletrônico** *oo keye-shuh uhleh-trau-nee-kau*
the bank	**o banco** *oo buhn-koo*
the currency exchange office	**o câmbio** *oo kuhm-bee-oo*
What time does the bank open/close?	**A que horas o banco abre/fecha?** *uh keh aw-ruhz oo buhn-koo ah-breh/feh-shuh*
I'd like to change dollars/pounds/euros into reais.	**Queria trocar dólares/libras/euros em reais.** *keh-ree-uh troo-kahr daw-luhrz/lee-bruhz/ehoo-rooz eng rree-eyez*

12

Currency exchange offices (**Câmbio**) can be found in most
Brazilian tourist centers; they generally stay open longer than
banks, especially during the summer season. Travel agencies and
hotels are other places where you can exchange money, but the rate
will not be as good. In heavy tourist areas, you can also find currency
exchange machines/ATMs on the streets. Of course, you should use
caution when exchanging/withdrawing money on the street, especially
in cities where crime rates are high. Remember to take your passport
with you when you want to change money.

I want to cash some traveler's checks [cheques].	**Quero trocar cheques de viagem.** *keh•roo troo•kahr sheh•kehz deh vee•ah•zseng*

For Numbers, see page 8.

Getting Around

How do I get to the city center?	**Como vou para o centro da cidade?** *kau•moo vawoo puh•ruh oo sehn•troo duh see•dahd*
Where's...?	**Onde é...?** *aund eh...*
the airport	**o aeroporto** *oo uh•eh•rau•paur•too*
the train station	**a estação ferroviária** *uh ee•stuh•sohm feh•rroo•vee•ah•ree•uh*
the bus station	**a estação de ônibus** *uh ee•stuh•sohm deh aw•nee•boos*

the metro [underground] station	**a estação de metrô**	uh ee-stuh-<u>sohm</u> deh <u>meh</u>-troo
How far is it?	**A que distância fica?**	uh keh dee-<u>stuhn</u>-see-uh <u>fee</u>-kuh
Where can I buy tickets?	**Onde posso comprar bilhetes?**	aund <u>paw</u>-soo kaum-<u>prahr</u> bee-<u>lyehtz</u>
A one-way/return-trip ticket to…	**Um bilhete de ida/de ida e volta para…**	oong bee-<u>lyeht</u> deh <u>ee</u>-thuh/deh <u>ee</u>-thuh ee <u>vaul</u>-tuh <u>puh</u>-ruh…
How much?	**Quanto custa?**	<u>kwuhn</u>-too <u>koo</u>-stuh
Are there any discounts?	**Há descontos?**	ah dehs-<u>caun</u>-tooz
Which…?	**Qual…?**	kwahl…
gate	**porta**	<u>port</u>-uh
line	**linha**	<u>lee</u>-nyuh
platform	**plataforma**	plah-tuh-<u>fawr</u>-muh
Where can I get a taxi?	**Onde posso pegar um táxi?**	aund <u>paw</u>-soo peh-<u>gahr</u> oong <u>tahk</u>-see
Please take me to this address.	**Leve-me neste endereço.**	<u>leh</u>-veh-meh nehst ehn-deh-<u>reh</u>-soo

14

| Where can I rent a car? | **Onde posso alugar um carro?** *aund paw•soo uh•loo•gahr oong kah•rroo* |
| Could I have a map? | **Pode me dar um mapa?** *pawd meh dahr oong mah•puh* |

Tickets

When's…to…?	**A que horas é…para…?** *uh kee aw•ruhz eh… puh•ruh…*
the (first) bus	**o (primeiro) ônibus** *uh (pree•may•ruh) aw•nee•boos*
the (next) flight	**o (próximo) vôo** *oo (praw•see•moo) vau•oo*
the (last) train	**o (último) trem** *oo (ool•tee•moo) treng*
Where can I buy tickets?	**Onde posso comprar bilhetes?** *aund paw•soo kaum•prahr bee•lyehtz*

YOU MAY HEAR…

sempre em frente *sehm•preh eng frehn•teh*	straight ahead
à esquerda *ah ee•skehr•duh*	on the left
à direita *ah dee•ray•tuh*	on the right
depois da/ao dobrar a esquina *deh•poyz dah/ahoo doo•brahr uh ees•kee•nuh*	on/around the corner
em frente de *eng frehn•teh deh*	opposite
por trás de *poor trahz deh*	behind
a seguir ao *m*/à *f* *uh seh•geer ahoo/ah*	next to
depois do *m*/da *f* *deh•poyz thoo/duh*	after
norte/sul *nawrt/sool*	north/south
leste/oeste *lehs•the/aw•ehs•teh*	east/west
no semáforo *noo seh•mah•fau•roo*	at the traffic light
no cruzamento *noo croo•zuh•mehn•too*	at the intersection

Intercity buses are fairly cheap and comfortable, usually with air conditioning. If you are traveling overnight, look for **leitos**, buses with reclining seats, clean sheets and pillows. Tickets are available from bus stations (**rodoviárias**).

Car Hire

Where can I rent a car?	**Onde posso alugar um carro?**	*aund paw•soo uh•loo•gahr oong kah•rroo*
I'd like to rent...	**Queria alugar...**	*keh•ree•uh uh•loo•gahr...*
a cheap/small car	**um carro barato/pequeno**	*oong kah•rroo buh•rah•too/peh•keh•noo*
a 2-/4-door car	**um carro de duas/quatro portas**	*oong kah•rroo deh thoo•uhz/kwah•troo pawr•tuhz*
a(n) automatic/manual	**um carro automático/manual**	*oong kah•rroo awoo•too•mah•tee•koo/mah.noo.ahl*
a car with air conditioning	**um carro com ar condicionado**	*oong kah•rroo kaum ahr kawn•dee•seeoo•nah•thoo*
a car seat	**um assento de carro de bebê**	*oong uh•sehn•too deh kah•rroo deh beh•beh*
How much...	**Quanto é...?**	*kwuhn•too eh...*
per day/week	**por dia/semana**	*poor dee•uh/seh•muh•nuh*
per kilometer	**por quilômetro**	*poor kee•law•meh•troo*

Taxis are yellow in Rio de Janeiro and white in São Paulo. Fares are generally pretty cheap. All Brazilian taxis have meters, except in small towns. In this instance it is best to agree the fare with the driver in advance.

for unlimited mileage	**com quilometragem ilimitada** *kaum kee•lae•meh•trah•zseng ee•lee•mee•tah•thuh*
with insurance	**com seguro** *kaum seh•goo•roo*
Are there any discounts?	**Há descontos?** *ah dehs•kaum•tooz*

YOU MAY HEAR…

Tem uma carta de condução internacional? *teng oo•muh kahr•tuh deh kaum•doo•sohm een•tehr•nuh•see•oo•nahl*
Do you have an international driver's license?

O seu passaporte, por favor. *oo sehoo pah•suh•pawr•teh poor fuh•vaur*
Your passport, please.

Quer seguro? *kehr seh•goo•roo*
Do you want insurance?

É preciso deixar um sinal de… *eh preh•see•zoo day•shahr oong see•nahl deh…*
There is a deposit of…

Assine aqui, por favor. *uh•see•neh uh•kee poor fuh•vaur*
Please sign here.

Parking can be difficult in big cities. Always lock your car and never leave anything in sight (even if you consider it not valuable) as it can encourage break-ins. Parking "guards" tend to appear within seconds of parking your car, offering to watch over it for you for a (modest) fee. It is advisable to agree to this as otherwise you may risk returning to a slightly damaged vehicle. Licensed guards operate in Rio and São Paulo. They will issue a receipt that covers a set period of time.

Places to Stay

Can you recommend a hotel?	**Pode recomendar um hotel?** *pawd reh•kaw•mehn•dahr oong aw•tehl*
I have a reservation.	**Tenho uma reserva.** *teh•nyoo oo•muh reh•zehr•vuh*
My name is…	**Meu nome é…** *mehoo naum•eh eh…*
Do you have a room…?	**Tem um quarto…?** *teng oong kwahr•too…*
for one/two	**para um/dois** *puh•ruh oong/doyz*
with a bathroom	**com banheiro** *kaum buh•nyay•roo*

Rio drivers are especially notorious for their erratic lane-changing, in-town speeding and disregard for pedestrians and other drivers on the road. Be on the defensive and expect the unexpected. Speeding fines can be huge (several hundred dollars) even if going only slightly over the limit, which can change erratically. Be warned, it is polite to beep your horn when overtaking, and flashing your lights as a warning is common. It is illegal to drink and drive and there is a zero tolerance policy in operation. If in doubt, take a cab.

with air conditioning	**com ar condicionado** *kaum ar kawn•dee•seeoo•<u>nah</u>•thoo*
For…	**Para…** *puh•ruh…*
tonight	**hoje à noite** *auzseh <u>ah</u> noyt*
two nights	**duas noites** *<u>thoo</u>•uhz noytz*
one week	**uma semana** *<u>oo</u>•muh seh•<u>muh</u>•nuh*
How much is it?	**Quanto custa?** *<u>kwuhn</u>•too <u>koo</u>•stuh*
Do you have anything cheaper?	**Há mais barato?** *ah meyez buh•<u>rah</u>•too*
What time is check-out?	**A que horas temos de deixar o quarto?** *uh kee <u>aw</u>•ruhz <u>teh</u>•mooz deh thay•<u>shahr</u> oo <u>kwahr</u>•too*
Can I leave this in the safe?	**Posso deixar isto no cofre?** *<u>paw</u>•soo thay•<u>shahr</u> <u>ee</u>•stoo noo <u>kaw</u>•freh*
Can I leave my bags?	**Posso deixar a minha bagagem?** *<u>paw</u>•soo day•<u>shahr</u> uh <u>mee</u>•nyuh buh•<u>gah</u>•geng*
Can I have the bill/ a receipt?	**Pode me dar a conta/um recibo?** *pawd meh <u>dahr</u> uh <u>kaum</u>•tuh/oong reh•<u>see</u>•boo*
I'll pay in cash/by credit card.	**Pago com dinheiro/com o cartão de crédito.** *<u>pah</u>•goo kaum dee•<u>nyay</u>•roo/kaum oo kuhr•<u>tohm</u> deh <u>kreh</u>•dee•too*

21

In Brazil, the cheapest place to stay is the **dormitório**, providing a shared room for a few **reais** per night. Other kinds of lodging include:

Hotel In Brazil, most hotels are regulated by **Embratur** (the Brazilian Tourism Authority). There are five official categories.

Hotel-Apartamento Apartment hotels ranging from 2- to 4-star.

Hotel fazenda Farmhouse lodges, generally equipped with a swimming pool, tennis court and horseback-riding facilities.

Pousada A state-owned inn converted from an old castle, monastery, convent, palace or in a location of interest to tourists.

Pensão Corresponds to a boarding house. Usually divided into four categories.

Pousada de juventude Youth hostel; there are over 90 youth hostels in Brazil, which are open to anyone, regardless of age, though members can obtain discounts. Hostels are extremely popular and the best ones book up quickly so it is best to book these in advance.

Residencial Bed and breakfast accommodations.

Communications

Where's an internet café?	**Onde fica um internet café?** _aund_ _fee_·kuh oong een·tehr·_neht_ kuh·_feh_
Can I access the Internet here?	**Tenho acesso à internet aqui?** _teh_·nyoo uh·_seh_·soo ah een·tehr·_neht_ uh·_kee_
Can I check email here?	**Posso ler o meu e-mail aqui?** _paw_·soo lehr oo mehoo ee·_mehl_ uh·_khee_
How much per (half) hour?	**Quanto é por (meia) hora?** _kwuhn_·too eh poor (_may_·uh) _aw_·ruh
How do I connect/ log on?	**Como conecto/faço o logon?** _kau_·moo koo·_nehk_·too/_fah_·soo oo _law_·gawn

A phone card, please.	**Um cartão telefónico, por favor.** *oong kuhr·tohm tehl·eh·fawn·ee·koo poor fuh·vaur*
Can I have your phone number?	**Pode me dar o seu número de telefone?** *pawd meh dahr oo sehoo noo·meh·roo deh tehl·fawn*
Here's my number/ email address.	**Este é o meu número/e-mail.** *ehst eh oo mehoo noo·meh·roo/ee·mehl*
Call me.	**Telefone-me.** *tehl·fawn·eh·meh*
Email me.	**Envie um e-mail.** *ehn·vee·eh oong ee·mehl*
Hello. This is…	**Alô. Meu nome é…** *aw·lah. Mehoo naum·eh eh…*
I'd like to speak to…	**Queria falar com…** *keh·ree·uh fuh·lahr kaum…*
Could you repeat that, please?	**Poderia repetir, por favor?** *poh·deh·ree·ah reh·peh·teer poor fuh·vaur*

Payphones are easy to use but you will need to purchase a pre-paid calling card. You can buy these from any store displaying a sign reading **Cartão Telefônico Aqui**. Temporary mobile phones with 'pay as you go' plans are also available. The Brazilian internet market is huge and internet cafes can be found throughout the country, although connections in smaller beach resorts can be slow. Many larger hotels provide free WiFi.

I'll call back later.	**Chamo mais tarde.** _shuh_•moo meyez _tahr_•deh
Bye.	**Tchau.** Cha•oo
Where's the post office?	**Onde são os correios?** aund sohm ooz koo•_rray_•ooz
I'd like to send this to…	**Gostaria de mandar isto para…** goo•stuh•_ree_•uh deh muhn•_dahr_ ee•stoo _puh_•ruh…
check e-mail	**tjekke min e-mail** _tjay_•ker meen _ee_•mail
print	**printe** _prin_•ter
plug in/charge my laptop/iPhone/ iPad/BlackBerry?	**oplade min bærbare/iPhone/iPad/BlackBerry?** ohb•la•der meen behr•barer/iPhone/iPad/BlackBerry
access Skype?	**bruge Skype?** broo•er Skype
What is the WiFi password?	**Hvad er WiFi-passwordet?** vadh her WiFi-pass•word•edh
Is the WiFi free?	**Er der gratis WiFi?** ehr dehr ghra•tis WiFi
Do you have bluetooth?	**Har I bluetooth?** hahr ee bluetooth?
Do you have a scanner?	**Har I en scanner?** hah ee ehn scan•ner

24

Social Media

Are you on Facebook/Twitter?	**Está no Facebook/Twitter?** *ee‑stah noo facebook/twitter*
What's your username?	**Qual é o seu nome de usuário?** *kwahl eh oo sehoo <u>naum</u>‑eh deh <u>oo</u>‑ zuh‑ah‑<u>ree</u>‑uh*
I'll add you as a friend.	**Vou adicioná‑lo como amigo.** *vawoo‑oo uh‑dee‑seeoo‑<u>nah</u>‑loo kau‑<u>moo</u> uh‑<u>mee</u>‑goo*
I'll follow you on Twitter.	**Vou segui‑lo no Twitter.** *vawoo‑oo seh‑<u>gee</u>‑loo noo Twitter*
Are you following…?	**Está seguindo…?** *ee‑stah uh seh‑<u>gheeng</u>‑doo…*
I'll put the pictures on Facebook/Twitter.	**Vou colocar as fotos no Facebook/Twitter.** *vawoo koo‑<u>loo</u>‑khahr uhz faw‑tawz noo Facebook/Twitter*
I'll tag you in the pictures.	**Vou te marcar nas fotos.** *vawoo tee‑mahr‑<u>kahr</u> nuhz faw‑<u>tawz</u>*

Conversation

Hello.	**Oi.** <u>*au*</u>*‑hee*
How are you?	**Tudo bem?** *Too‑duh beng*
Fine, thanks.	**Bem, obrigado *m*/obrigada *f*.** *behm aw‑bree‑<u>gah</u>‑doo/aw‑bree‑<u>gah</u>‑duh*
Excuse me!	**Desculpe!** *dehz‑<u>kool</u>‑peh*
Do you speak English?	**Fala inglês?** <u>*fah*</u>*‑luh eeng‑<u>lehz</u>*
What's your name?	**Como se chama?** *kau‑moo seh <u>shuh</u>‑muh*
My name is…	**Meu nome é…** *mehoo <u>naum</u>‑ee eh…*
Nice to meet you.	**Muito prazer.** <u>*mooee*</u>*‑too pruh‑<u>zehr</u>*
Where are you from?	**De onde é?** *deh aund eh*
I'm from the U.S./U.K.	**Sou dos Estados Unidos/da Inglaterra.** *soh dooz ee‑<u>stah</u>‑dooz oo‑<u>nee</u>‑dooz/ duh eeng‑luh‑<u>teh</u>‑rruh*
What do you do?	**O que é que faz?** *oo kee eh keh fahz*
I work for…	**Trabalho para…** *truh‑<u>bah</u>‑lyoo <u>puh</u>‑ruh…*

I'm a student.	**Sou estudante.** *sauoo ee·stoo·<u>duhnt</u>*
I'm retired.	**Sou aposentado *m*/aposentada *f*.**
	soh uh·poo·zehn·<u>tah</u>·doo/uh·poo·zehn·<u>tah</u>·duh
Do you like…?	**Gosta de…?** *<u>gaw</u>·stuh deh…*
Goodbye.	**Tchau.** *chah·oo*
See you later.	**Até mais tarde.** *uh·<u>teh</u> meyez tahrd*

Romance

| Would you like to go out for a drink/dinner? | **Quer tomar uma bebida/comer fora?** *<u>kehr</u> too·<u>mahr</u> oo·muh beh·<u>bee</u>·thuh/<u>koo</u>·mehr <u>faw</u>·ruh* |

In Brazil, a standard greeting is a handshake accompanied by direct eye contact and the appropriate greeting for the time of day. Once a closer relationship has developed, greetings become more personal: men may greet each other with a hug, and women kiss each other twice on the cheek starting on the right-hand side. Brazilians often use a first name with a title of respect: **Senhor** for men, **Senhora** or **Dona** for women. Wait until invited before moving to a first-name basis.

What are your plans for tonight/tomorrow?	**Quais são os seus planos para hoje à noite/amanhã?** kweyez sohm ooz sehooz _pluh_•nooz _puh_•ruh auzseh ah noyt/uh•muh•_nyuh_
Can I have your number?	**Qual o seu número de telefone?** Kwal oo seoh _noo_•meh•roo deh tehl•_fawn_
Can I join you?	**Posso te acompanhar?** _paw_•soo teh uh•kaum•puh•_nyahr_
Can I buy you a drink?	**O que quer beber?** oo keh kehr beh•_behr_
I like you.	**Gosto de você.** _gawzh_•too deh voh•seh
I love you.	**Te amo.** teh _uh_•moo

Accepting & Rejecting

I'd love to.	**Adoraria ir.** uh•doo•ruh•_ree_•uh eer
Where should we meet?	**Onde vamos nos encontrar?** aund _vuh_•mooz nooz ehng•kaun•_trahr_
I'll meet you at the bar/your hotel.	**Vou te encontrar no bar/hotel.** vauoo tee ehn•kaun•_trahr_ noo bahr/_aw_•tehl
I'll come by at…	**Eu passo por lá às…** ehoo _pah_•soo poor lah ahz…
What's your address?	**Qual é o suo endereço?** kwahl eh uh _soo_•uh ehn•deh•_reh_•soo
I'm busy.	**Mas tenho muito que fazer.** muhz _teh_•nyoo _mooee_•too keh fuh•_zehr_
I'm not interested.	**Não estou interessado _m_/interessada _f._** nohm ee•_stawoo_ een•treh•_sah_•thoo/een•treh•_sah_•thuh
Leave me alone.	**Me deixe em paz.** meh _day_•sheh eng pahz
Stop bothering me!	**Páre!** pah•_reeee_
Stop bothering me!	**Lad mig være i fred!** la mie _vay_•er ee frehdh

Food & Drink

Eating Out

Can you recommend a good restaurant/bar?	**Pode recomendar um bom restaurante/bar?** *pawd reh·kaw·mehn·dahr oong bohng reh·stahoo·ruhnt/bar*
Is there a(n) traditional/ inexpensive restaurant near here?	**Há um restaurante tradicional/barato perto daqui?** *ah oong reh·stuhoo·ruhnt truh·dee·see·oo·nahl/buh·rah·too pehr·too duh·kee*
A table for..., please.	**Uma mesa para..., por favor.** *oo·muh meh·zuh puh·ruh...poor fuh·vaur*
Could we sit...?	**Podemos sentar...?** *poo·deh·mooz sehn·tahr...*
here/there	**aqui/ali** *uh·kee/uh·lee*
outside	**lá fora** *lah faw·ruh*
in a non-smoking area	**na área para não-fumantes** *nuh ah·ree·uh puh·ruh noh-foo·muhnts*
I'm waiting for someone.	**Estou à espera de alguém.** *ee·stawoo ah ee·speh·ruh deh ahl·gehm*
Where's the restroom [toilet]?	**Onde são os banheiros?** *aund sohm ooz buh·nyay·rooz*

YOU MAY SEE...

COUVERT	cover charge
PREÇO-FIXO	fixed-price
CARDÁPIO	menu
CARDÁPIO DO DIA	menu of the day
SERVIÇO (NÃO) INCLUÍDO	service (not) included
ESPECIAIS	specials

A menu, please.	**Uma cardápio, por favor.**
	oong car•dah•pee•oo poor fuh•vaur
What do you recommend?	**O que é que me recomenda?** *oo keh eh keh meh reh•koo•mehn•duh*
I'd like...	**Queria...** *keh•ree•uh...*
Some more..., please.	**Mais..., por favor.** *meyez...poor fuh•vaur*
Enjoy your meal.	**Bom apetite.** *bohng uh•peh•tee•teh*
The check [bill], please.	**A conta, por favor.** *uh kaum•tuh poor fuh•vaur*
Is service included?	**O serviço está incluído?** *oo sehr•vee•soo ee•stah een•kloo•ee•thoo*
Can I pay by credit card?	**Posso pagar com cartão de crédito?** *paw•soo puh•gahr kaum kuhr•tohm deh kreh•dee•too*
Could I have a receipt, please?	**Pode me dar um recibo, por favor?** *pawd meh dahr oong reh•see•boo poor fuh•vaur*
Thank you.	**Obrigado m/Obrigada f.** *aw•bree•gah•thoo/aw•bree•gah•thuh*

Breakfast

o toucinho *oo taw•see•nyoo*	bacon
o pão *oo pohm*	bread
a manteiga *uh muhn•tay•guh*	butter
as carnes frias *uhz kahr•nehz free•uhz*	cold cuts [charcuterie]
o queijo *oo kay•zsoo*	cheese
o ovo... *oo au•voo...*	...egg
muito fervido/fervido macio *mooee•too fehr•vee•thoo/fehr•vee•thoo muh•see•oo*	hard-boiled/ soft-boiled
estrelado [frito] *ee•struh•lah•doo [free•too]*	fried
mexido *meh•shee•doo*	scrambled
a geleia *ah zseh•lay•uh*	jam
a omelete *uh aw•meh•leh•tuh*	omelet

O pequeno almoço

Breakfast is usually served from 7:00 to 10:00 a.m. It can include coffee, rolls, butter and jam, along with fresh fruit juice, fruit, toast and pastries.

O almoço

Lunch is the main meal of the day, served from 12:30 to 2:30 p.m. Shops are normally closed during these hours. In Brazilian resorts, lunch is often served without interruption from 12:30 until the evening. It generally includes soup or salad, fish or meat, and a dessert.

O jantar

Dinner is served from about 8:00 to 11:00 p.m. It typically includes soup, fish or meat, salad, bread, and fruit or a sweet for dessert. Coffee or espresso is almost always served at the end of the meal.

as torradas *uhz too•rrah•duhz*	toast
as salsichas *uhz sahl•see•shuhz*	sausages
o jogurte *oo yaw•goort*	yogurt

Appetizers

o pipis *oo pee•peez*	spicy chicken stew
as carnes frias *uhz kahr•nehz free•uhz*	cold cuts
siri recheada *see•ree eh•shee•ah•thuh*	stuffed crab
o paio *oo peye•oo*	smoked pork fillet
os pimentões assados *ooz pee•mehn•toehnz uh•sah•dooz*	roasted peppers
o chouriço *oo shauoo•ree•soo*	sausage
as lulas à milanesa *uhz loo•luhz ah mee•luh•neh•zuh*	squid

Meat

a carne de vaca *uh kahrn deh <u>vah</u>·kuh*	beef
o frango *oo <u>fruhn</u>·goo*	chicken
o carneiro *oo kuhr·<u>nay</u>·roo*	lamb
a carne de porco *uh kahrn deh <u>paur</u>·koo*	pork
o bife [filé] *oo beef [fee·<u>leh</u>]*	steak
a vitela *uh vee·<u>tehl</u>·uh*	veal

YOU MAY HEAR...

malpassado *mal·pass·sah·doh*	rare
ao ponto *uhoo pon·toh*	medium
bem passado *beng pass·sah·doh*	well-done

Fish & Seafood

o pargo *oo <u>pahr</u>·goo*	bream
a lampreia *uh luhm·<u>pray</u>·uh*	lamprey
a lagosta *uh luh·<u>gau</u>·stuh*	lobster
o polvo *oo <u>paul</u>·voo*	octopus

a canjica *uh kuhn·zsee·kuh*	dessert made with sweet corn and milk
a goiabada *uh goy·uh·bah·duh*	thick paste made of guavas
a mousse de maracujá *uh moo·seh deh muh·ruh·koo·zsah*	passion fruit mousse
os ovos moles *ooz aw·vooz mawlz*	egg yolks cooked in syrup
o pastel de Tentúgal *oo puhz·tehl deh tehn·too·gahl*	pastry filled with egg yolks cooked in syrup
pudim *poo·deeng*	caramel custard
quindim *keeng·deeng*	coconut and egg yolk pudding

Drinks

The wine list/drink menu, please.	**A carta de vinhos/cardápio de bebidas, por favor.** *uh kahr·tuh deh vee·nyooz/car·dah·pee·oo deh beh·bee·duhz poor fuh·vaur*

Brazil turns out some good red and white wines from its vineyards in the South. Labels to look for include **Almadén** and **Forestier**.

What do you recommend?	**O que me recomenda?** *oo keh meh reh•koo•mehn•duh*
I'd like a bottle/glass of red/white wine.	**Queria uma garrafa/um copo de vinho tinto/branco.** *keh•ree•uh oo•muh guh•rrah•fuh/oong kaw•poo deh vee•nyoo teen•too/bruhn•koo*
The house wine, please.	**O vinho da casa, por favor.** *oo vee•nyoo duh kah•zuh poor fuh•vaur*
Another bottle/glass, please.	**Outra garrafa/Outro copo, por favor.** *auoo•truh guh•rrah•fuh/auoo•troo kaw•poo poor fuh•vaur*
I'd like a local beer.	**Gostaria de uma cerveja local.** *goo•stuh•ree•uh deh oo•muh sehr•vay•zsuh loo•kahl*
Can I buy you a drink?	**Posso oferecer uma bebida?** *paw•soo aw•freh•sehr oo•muh beh•bee•thuh*
Cheers!	**Saúde!** *Sah•ood*
A coffee/tea, please.	**Um café/chá, por favor.** *oong kuh•feh/shah poor fuh•vaur*

Look for the bars advertising **suco** (juice) with lots of fresh fruit on display. **Sumol**® is the oldest brand name of fruit juice and is found in almost every shop selling food. It is a lightly carbonated orange drink.

Black.	**Cafezinho.** kuh·feh·<u>zee</u>·nyoo
With...	**com...** kaum...
milk	**leite** layt
sugar	**açúcar** uh·<u>soo</u>·kuhr
artificial sweetener	**adoçante** uh·doo·<u>suhnty</u>
A..., please.	**..., por favor.** ...por fuh·<u>vaur</u>
juice	**Um suco** oong <u>soo</u>·koo
soda	**Um refrigerante** oong reh·<u>freh</u>·zhay·rahnt
sparkling/still	**Uma água com/sem gás** <u>oo</u>·muh <u>ah</u>·gwuh
water	kaum/sehm gahz
Is the tap water safe to drink?	**A água da torneira é boa para beber?** uh <u>ah</u>·gwuh duh toor·<u>nay</u>·ruh eh <u>baw</u>·uh <u>puh</u>·ruh beh·<u>behr</u>

Beer is a popular drink in Brazil. Try local brew **Antártica**. It is often served with **tremoços** (salted lupini beans) or **amendoins** (peanuts). **Cachaça** is the national spirit and comes in varying degrees of quality. It is made from the juice of cane sugar. The very best compare favorably to a top whiskey or brandy. The famous **caipirinha** cocktail is based on this.

Leisure Time

Sightseeing

Where's the tourist office?	**Onde é o posto de informações turísticas?** *aund eh oo pau•stoo deh een•foor•muh•soings too•ree•stee•kuhz*
What are the main points of interest?	**O que há de mais interessante para se ver?** *oo kee ah deh meyez een•tehr•reh•suhnt puh•ruh seh vehr*
Do you have tours in English?	**Tem excursões em inglês?** *teng ee•skoor•soings eng eng•lehz*
Can I have a map/guide?	**Pode me dar um mapa/guia?** *pawd meh dahr oong mah•puh/gee•uh*

Shopping

Where is the market/mall [shopping?	**Onde é o mercado/o centro comercial?** *aund eh oo mehr•kah•thoo/oo sehn•troo koo•mehr•see•ahl*
I'm just looking.	**Estou só vendo.** *ee•stawoo saw vehn•doo*
Can you help me?	**Pode me ajudar?** *pawd meh uh•zsoo•dahr*
I'm being helped.	**Alguém está me ajudando.** *ahl•gehng ee•stah uh meh uh•zsoo•dahd•doh*
How much is it?	**Quanto é?** *kwuhn•too eh*

YOU MAY SEE...

HORÁRIO DE ABERTURA	opening hours
FECHADO PARA ALMOÇO	closed for lunch
PROVADOR	fitting room
CAIXA	cashier
SÓ DINHEIRO	cash only
CARTÕES DE CRÉDITO ACEITES	credit cards accepted

That one, please.	**Aquele *m*/Aquela *f*, por favor.** uh•<u>kehl</u>/uh•<u>keh</u>•luh poor fuh•<u>vaur</u>
That's all, thanks.	**Étudo, obrigado *m*/obrigada *f*.** eh <u>too</u>•doo aw•bree•<u>gah</u>•doo/aw•bree•<u>gah</u>•thuh
Where can I pay?	**Onde pago?** aund <u>pah</u>•goo
I'll pay in cash/ by credit card.	**Pago com dinheiro/com o cartão de crédito.** <u>pah</u>•goo kaum dee•<u>nyay</u>•roo/kaum oo kuhr•<u>tohm</u> deh <u>kreh</u>•dee•too
A receipt, please.	**Um recibo, por favor.** oong reh•<u>see</u>•boo poor fuh•<u>vaur</u>

International credit cards are generally accepted. The most commonly used cards are Visa™, American Express®, Europay/ Mastercard™, JCB and Maestro®. In some small villages and towns cash may still be the only form of currency accepted.

Sport & Leisure

When's the game?	**Quando é o jogo?** _kwuhn_•doo eh o _zsau_•goo
Where's…?	**Onde é…?** _aund eh…_
the beach	**a praia** uh _preye_•uh
the park	**o parque** oo _pahr_•keh
the pool	**a piscina** uh pee•_see_•nuh
Is it safe to swim here?	**Pode nadar aqui sem perigo?** pawd nuh•_dahr_ uh•_kee_ sehn peh•_ree_•goo
Can I hire golf clubs?	**Posso alugar tacos?** _paw_•soo uh•loo•_gahr_ tah•kooz
How much per hour?	**Qual é a tarifa por hora?** kwahl eh uh tuh•_ree_•fuh poor _aw_•ruh
How far is it to…?	**A que distância fica…?** uh keh dee•_stuhn_•see•uh _fee_•kuh…
Can you show me on the map?	**Pode indicar no mapa?** pawd een•dee•_kahr_ noo _mah_•puh

Brazilians are avid soccer fans and the sport unites all ages and classes. Rio boasts Maracanã, the largest soccer stadium in the world. Be warned, during World Cup season, the country grinds to a halt!

Going Out

What is there to do in the evenings?	**O que há para se fazer à noite?** *oo keh ah <u>puh</u>•ruh seh fuh•<u>zehr</u> ah noyt*
Do you have a program of events?	**Tem um programa dos espectáculos?** *teng oong proo•<u>gruh</u>•muh dooz ee•spehk•<u>tah</u>•koo•looz*
What's playing at the movies [cinema] tonight?	**O que está passando no cinema hoje à noite?** *oo kee ee•<u>stah</u> pah•san•doh noo see•<u>neh</u>•muh auzeh ah noyt*
Where's…?	**Onde é…?** *aund eh…*
the downtown area	**o centro** *oo <u>sehn</u>•troo*
the bar	**o bar** *oo bar*
the dance club	**a discoteca** *uh deez•koo•<u>teh</u>•kuh*
Is there a cover charge?	**É preciso pagar entrada [ingresso]?** *eh preh•<u>see</u>•zoo puh•<u>gahr</u> ehn•<u>trah</u>•duh [een•<u>greh</u>•soo]*

Carnaval is widely celebrated in Brazil. A time of lavish celebration before Lent, **Carnaval** begins four days before Ash Wednesday, and ends with the famous 'Fat Tuesday' celebration. Look for parades on the streets and carnival balls (**bailes carnavalescos**). The famed **Carnaval do Rio** sees the spectacularly colorful competition between the various samba schools in a parade through the streets of Rio de Janeiro.

Samba and **bossa nova** are the dance styles best known abroad, but look out for regional rhythms like **pagode**, **lambada**, **frevo**, **forró**, **maracatu**, **baião**, **carimbó** and **bumba-meu boi**, with their mixture of African, Indian, and European influences.

Baby Essentials

Do you have…?	**Tem…?** *teng…*
a baby bottle	**uma mamadeira** *oo·muh muh·muh·<u>deh</u>·rah*
baby wipes	**os lenços umedecidos para o bebê [nenê]** *ooz lehn·<u>sawz</u> oo·muh·duh·<u>see</u>·duhz <u>puh</u>·ruh oo beh·<u>beh</u> [neh·<u>neh</u>]*
a car seat	**um assento de carro** *oong uh·<u>sehn</u>·too deh <u>kah</u>·rroo*
a children's menu/ portion	**uma porção de criança** *oo·muh poor·<u>sohm</u> deh kree·<u>uhn</u>·suh*
a child's seat	**uma cadeirinha de criança** *<u>oo</u>·muh kuh·day·<u>ree</u>·nyuh deh kree·<u>uhn</u>·suh*
a crib	**uma cama de bebê [neném]** *oo·muh <u>kuh</u>·muh deh beh·<u>beh</u> [neh·<u>neh</u>]*
diapers [nappies]	**as fraldas** *uhz <u>frahl</u>·duhz*
formula	**fórmula de bebê [neném]** *<u>fawr</u>·moo·luh deh beh·<u>beh</u> [neh·<u>neh</u>]*
a pacifier [dummy]	**uma chupeta** *<u>oo</u>·muh shoo·<u>peh</u>·tuh*
a playpen	**um parque para crianças** *oong pahr·<u>kuh</u> puh·ruh kree·<u>uhn</u>·suhz*
a stroller [pushchair]	**uma cadeira de bebê [neném]** *<u>oo</u>·muh kuh·day·<u>ruh</u> deh beh·<u>beh</u> [neh·<u>neh</u>]*

Can I breastfeed the baby here?	**Posso amamentar o bebê [neném] aqui?** *paw·soo uh·muh·mehn·tahr oo beh·beh [neh·neh] uh·kee*
Where can I change the baby?	**Onde posso trocar o bebê [neném]?** *aund paw·soo traw·kahr oo beh·beh [neh·neh]*

For Eating Out, see page 28.

Disabled Travelers

Is there...?	**Há...?** *ah...*
access for the disabled	**acesso para deficientes físicos** *uh·seh·soo puh·ruh deh·fee·see·ehntz fee·see·kooz*
a wheelchair ramp	**uma rampa de cadeira de rodas** *oo·muh ruhm·puh deh kuh·day·ruh deh raw·thuhz*
a handicapped- [disabled-] accessible toilet	**um banheiro acessível para deficientes** *oong buh·nyay·rooz uh·seh·see·vehl puh·ruh deh·fee·see·ehntz*
I need...	**Preciso de...** *preh·see·zoo deh...*
assistance	**assistência** *uh·see·stehn·see·uh*
an elevator [lift]	**um elevador** *oong eh·leh·vuh·daur*
a ground-floor room	**um quarto no primeiro andar** *oong kwahr·too noo pree·may·roo uhn·dahr*

Health & Emergencies

Emergencies

Help!	**Socorro!** *soo•kau•rroo*
Go away!	**Vá embora!** *vah ehng•baw•ruh*
Call the police!	**Chame a polícia!** *shuh•meh uh poo•lee•see•uh*
Stop thief!	**Pare o ladrão!** *pah•ree oo luh•drohm*
Get a doctor!	**Chame um médico!** *shuh•meh oong meh•dee•koo*
Fire!	**Fogo!** *fau•goo*

YOU MAY HEAR…

Preencha este formulário.
pree•eng•sheh eh•stuh fawr•muh•lah•reeoo

Fill out this form.

A sua identificação, por favor. *uh soo•uh ee•dehnt•tee•fee•kuh•sohm por fuh•vaur*

Your identification, please.

Quando/Onde é que foi? *kwuhn•doo/ aund eh keh foy*

When/Where did it happen?

Como é ele/ela? *kau•moo eh ehleh/ehluh*

What does he/ she look like?

| I'm lost. | **Estou perdido** *m*/**perdida** *f*. *ee-stawoo* *pehr-dee-thoo/pehr-dee-thuh* |
| Can you help me? | **Pode me ajudar?** *pawd meh uh-zsoo-dahr* |

Health

I'm sick [ill].	**Estou doente.** *ee-stawoo doo-ehnt*
I need an English-speaking doctor.	**Preciso de um médico que fale inglês.** *preh-see-zoo deh oong meh-dee-koo keh fah-leh eeng-lehz*
It hurts here.	**Dói aqui.** *doy uh-kee*
I have a stomachache.	**Tenho dor de estômago.** *teh-nyoo daur deh ee-stau-muh-goo*
Where's the pharmacy [chemist]?	**Onde fica a farmácia?** *aund fee-kuh uh fuhr-mah-see-uh*
I'm pregnant.	**Estou grávida.** *ee-stawoo grah-vee-thuh*
I'm on…	**Estou tomando…** *ee-stawoo to-muhn-doo…*

In an emergency, dial **190** for the police, **192** for the ambulance, and **193** for the fire brigade.

Dictionary

A

accommodation o alojamento
adaptor o adaptador
address o endereço
after-sun lotion a loção pós-sol
age a idade
also também
and e
another outro, outra
ask pedir

B

baby o bebê [neném]; **~sitter** baby-sitter [a babá]; **~wipes** os lenços umedecidos para o bebê [neném]
baby bottle a mamadeira
backpack a mochila
bad mau, má
bathroom o banheiro
be v ser; **~ (temporary state)** estar; **~ (location)** ficar
beach a praia
beautiful bonito, bonita
because porque; **~ of** por causa de
bed a cama; **~ and breakfast** pousada [pernoite e café da manhã]
bedroom o quarto (de dormir)
bee a abelha
before antes de
beginner o/a principiante
better melhor
between entre

big grande
bird o pássar
bite (insect) a picada (de inseto)
blue azul
boat o barco
book *n* o livro; *v* reservar
border a fronteira
boring entediante
boy o menino
boyfriend o namorado
bra o sutiã
bread o pão
breakfast o café da manhã
Britain a Grã-Bretanha
British britânico
brother o irmão
brown o castanho
brush a escova
bus o ônibus; ~ **(long-distance)** o ônibus; ~ **station** a estação rodoviária; ~ **stop** a parada de ônibus
but mas
buy *v* comprar
bye adeus [tchau]

C

cable car o funicular; o teleférico
cake o bolo
call *v* chamar
car o carro; ~ **hire [BE]** aluguel de carros; ~ **park [BE]** o parque de estacionamento; ~ **rental** aluguel de carros

card o cartão ; **ATM** ~ o cartão eletrônico; **credit** ~ o cartão de crédito; **debit** ~ o cartão de débito; **phone** ~ o cartão de telefônico

cash o dinheiro

cat o gato [a gata]

change *n* **(coins)** troco (moeda); ~ *v* **(bus)** mudar (de ônibus); ~ *v* **(clothes)** trocar (de roupa); ~ *v* **(money)** trocar dinheiro; ~ *v* **(reservation)** mudar a reserva

changing rooms os vestiários

charge a tarifa

cheap barato

check (bill) a conta; **put it on the** ~ ponha na conta

check out *v* **(hotel)** pagar a conta; **(supermarket)** o caixa

cheers saúde

cheese o queijo

child a criança

chips [BE] as batatas fritas

cigarette o cigarro

cigars os charutos

clean *adj* limpo [limpa]

close *v* fechar

clubs (golf) os tacos de golfe

coast a costa

coat o casaco [comprido]

cockroach a barata

coffee o café

coin a moeda

cold frio; ~ **(illness)** o resfriado

complain reclamar

conditioner (hair) o condicionador para o cabelo

condom o preservativo

directory (telephone) a lista telefônica
dirty sujo, suja
disabled (person) o/a deficiente
disconnect (computer) desligar [desconectar]
discount o desconto
dish (meal) o prato
dishes a louça
dishwashing liquid o detergente para a louça
dive v mergulhar
divorced divorciado
doctor o médico
dog o cão
doll a boneca
dollar (U.S.) o dólar
domestic (flight) doméstico
door a porta
double bed a cama de casal
double room o quarto de casal
down abaixo
downstairs em baixo
downtown o centro da cidade
dozen dúzia
dress n (clothing) vestido
drink n bebida
drinking water água potável
drive v conduzir
driver's license a carteira de motorista
drugstore a farmácia
drunk o bêbado
dry cleaner a lavanderia de limpeza a seco
during durante

dusty empoeirado
duty (tax) imposto
duty-free goods a mercadoria isenta de impostos
duty-free shopping as compras duty-free

E

ear o ouvido
ear drops gotas para os ouvidos
earlier mais cedo
early cedo
earrings os brincos
east leste
easy fácil
eat comer
empty *adj* vazio [vazia]
end *v* terminar
England a Inglaterra
English inglês
enjoy *v* apreciar
enough bastante [suficiente]
euro o euro
Europe a Europa
except exceto
excess o excesso
exchange *v* trocar
excursion a excursão
excuse me (apology) desculpe-me; **(to get attention)** com licença
exhausted *adj* exausto [exausta]
exhibition a exposição
exit a saída
expensive caro

expiration date a data de validade
extremely extremamente
eye o olho

F

face a cara; o rosto
facial a limpeza de pele
family a família
famous famoso
fan (electric) o ventilador
far longe
fare o bilhete
farm a fazenda
fast depressa
faster mais rápido
fast food as refeições rápidas
fat *n* a gordura; *adj* gordo
fat-free sem gordura
father o pai
faucet a torneira
favorite o preferido, a preferida
fax *n* o fax
fax *v* enviar fax
fear o medo
feed *v* alimentar
female a mulher
ferry a balsa
few poucos
fever a febre
fill out *v* **(form)** preencher
film (camera) o filme

fine (penalty) a multa
fire *n* o fogo
fire alarm o alarme de incêndio
fire department [brigade] o corpo de bombeiros
fire escape a saída de incêndio
fire extinguisher o extintor de incêndio
first o primeiro
first class a primeira classe
first-aid kit o estojo de primeiros socorros
fit (clothes) servir
fitting room o provador
fix *v* consertar
flag a bandeira
flash (photography) o flash
flashlight a lanterna
flat (tire) o furo (no pneu)
flight o vôo
floor (level) o andar
flower a flor
fly (insect) a mosca
fly *v* voar
food a comida
football [BE] o futebol
forecast a previsão
foreign o estrangeiro; ~ **currency** as moedas estrangeiras
forest a floresta
forget *v* esquecer
fork (utensil) o garfo; ~ **(in road)** a bifurcação
form o formulário
formula (baby) a papa
fortunately felizmente

fountain a fonte
free (available) livre; ~ **(no charge)** grátis
frequently muitas vezes, frequentemente
fresh fresco
friend o amigo, a amiga
full cheio

G

game o jogo
garage a garagem [a oficina mecânica]
garbage bag o saco de lixo
gasoline a gasolina
gate (airport) o portão
genuine autêntico, autêntica
get out v sair
gift a oferta
girl a menina
girlfriend a namorada
give v dar
glass (drinking) o copo
glass (material) o vidro
go ir
good bom [boa]; ~ **morning** bom dia;
~**night** boa noite
goodbye adeus
gram o grama
grandparent o avô, a avó
grape a uva
gray o cinza
green o verde
grocery store a mercearia

ground (camping) o terreno
group o grupo
guide (person) o/a guia

H

hair o cabelo; ~ **gel** o gel para o cabelo; ~**brush** a escova de cabelo; ~**dryer**
o secador de cabelo; ~**spray** o spray para o cabelo
haircut o corte de cabelo
hand cream o creme para as mãos
handbag [BE] a bolsa
handicapped o/a deficiente
handicapped accessible acessível a deficientes
hangover a ressaca
happy feliz
hat o chapéu
have *v* ter
head a cabeça
hear *v* ouvir
hearing aid o aparelho auditivo
heater o aquecedor
heating [BE] aquecimento
heavy pesado
hello oi, olá
help *n* a ajuda; *v* ajudar
home a casa
hot (temperature) quente; **(spicy)** picante
hour a hora
house a casa
hurt *adj* o ferido, a ferida
husband o marido

I

ice o gelo
ice cream o sorvete; **~ parlor** a sorveteria; **~ cone** o cone de sorvete
ill *adj* o/a doente
illness a doença
in (place) no; **(time)** em
information a informação
innocent o/a inocente
insect o inseto; **~ bite** a picada de inseto; **~ repellent** o repelente de insetos
insurance o seguro; **~ card** a apólice de seguro
introduce *v* introduzir
invite *v* convidar
Ireland a Irlanda
island a ilha

J

jeans as calças jeans
jellyfish a água-viva
jewelry as joias
joke a piada

K

key a chave
key card o cartão da porta
kiss beijar
knee o joelho

L

large grande
last o último
later mais tarde
learn *v* aprender

leather o couro
leave *v* partir
left a esquerda
less menos
lesson a lição
lighter o isqueiro
little pequeno, pequena
live *v* viver
log on *v* autenticar
log off *v* sair
long comprido; **(time)** muito
look *v* ver
lost *adj* perdido
lotion a loção
louder mais alto
love (a person) amar; **(a thing)** gostar de
lunch o almoço

M

man o homem
married casado
maybe talvez
meal a refeição
mean *v* significar
meat a carne
medicine o remédio
medium (size) médio; **(cooked)** ao ponto
meet *v* encontrar(-se)
menu o menu, o cardápio
message a mensagem
migraine a enxaqueca

miss *v* perder
missing em falta
mistake o engano, o erro
misunderstanding o mal-entendido
more mais
mother a mãe
motorway [BE] a estrada, a rodovia
much muito
mugging o assalto
museum o museu

N

nail (body) a unha; ~**polish** o esmalte de unhas
name o nome
nausea a náusea
near perto
nearest mais próximo
necessary necessário
new novo, nova
newspaper o jornal
next próximo, próxima
next to ao lado de
no não
noisy barulhento
none nenhum, nenhuma
north o norte
nothing nada
now agora
number plate (car) [BE] a placa do carro
nurse o enfermeiro, a enfermeira

O

often muitas vezes
oil o óleo
old o velho, a velha
one um, uma
open *v* abrir
open *adj* aberto, aberta
opposite o oposto
optician o oculista, oftalmologista
orange (fruit) a laranja; **(color)** laranja
order *v* encomendar
outdoor ao ar livre; ~ **pool** a piscina ao ar livre
outside fora de
over sobre
overdone *adj* cozido demais
overnight só uma noite

P

pacifier a chupeta
pain a dor
park *v* estacionar
parking o estacionamento; ~ **lot** o parque de estacionamento;
~ **meter** o parquímetro; ~ **space** a vaga de estacionamento
partner o companheiro, a companheira
party a festa
pay *v* pagar
pen a caneta
pencil o lápis
per por: ~ **day** por dia; ~ **hour** por hora;
~ **night** por noite; ~ **week** por semana
phone o telefone; ~ **call** o telefonema; ~ **card** o cartão telefônico

pink cor-de-rosa
plane o avião
play v jogar; **(instrument)** tocar
please por favor
plug (electric) a tomada (eléctrica)
plunger o desentupidor
pocket o bolso
poison o veneno
police a polícia; ~ **report** o boletim de ocorrência da polícia;
~ **station** a delegacia da polícia
pool a piscina
post [BE] o correio; ~ **office** os correios
pottery a cerâmica
pound (British sterling) a libra (esterlina)
pregnant a grávida
prescription a receita
press v **(clothing)** passar a ferro [engomar]
pretty bonito, bonita
print v imprimir
problem o problema

Q

quality a qualidade
question a pergunta
queue [BE] n a fila
quiet sossegado, sossegada

R

railway station [BE] a estação de caminhos de ferro [a estação ferroviária]
rain v chover
rape o estupro
razor a navalha; ~ **blade** a lâmina de barbear

read v ler
ready pronto, pronta
red vermelho, vermelha
refrigerator a geladeira
rent v alugar
rental car o carro alugado
reserve v reservar
restaurant o restaurante
restroom o banheiro
return v **(come back)** voltar; **(give back)** devolver
right (correct) certo; ~ **of way** prioridade
ring o anel
river o rio
road a estrada
robbed roubado, roubada
romantic romântico
room o quarto; ~ **service** o serviço de quarto
round-trip de ida e volta
rubbish [BE] o lixo; ~ **bin [BE]** a lata de lixo, lixeira

S

same o mesmo, a mesma
sand a areia
sandals as sandálias
sanitary napkin [pad] o papel higiênica
scarf o lenço , a echarpe (de pescoço)
school a escola
scissors a tesoura
sea o mar
shampoo o shampoo [o xampú]
sharp afiado, afiada

shaving cream o creme da barba
sheet o lençol
shirt a camisa
shoe o sapato; ~ **store** a sapataria
shopping compras; ~ **area** a zona comercial; ~ **centre [BE]** o centro comercial; ~ **mall** o shopping center
shower o chuveiro
sick doente
single (not married) solteiro; ~ **room** o quarto individual
sister a irmã
slow lento, lenta
small pequeno, pequena
snack bar a lanchonete, a cafetaria
sneakers os tênis
soccer o futebol
sock a meia
soft drink (soda) o refrigerante
sold out esgotada, esgotado
someone alguém

sometimes às vezes
son o filho
sorry desculpe
south sul
speak falar
sting a picada
stop *n* **(bus, tram)** a parada
straight ahead sempre em frente
street a estrada
study *v* estudar
subway o metrô; ~ **station** a estação de metrô
suitcase a mala de viagem

sun o sol

sun block o protetor solar

sunburn a queimadura de sol

sunglasses os óculos de sol

supermarket o supermercado

sweatshirt o agasalho, a blusa de moleton

sweet (taste) doce

swim *v* nadar

swimsuit o maiô de banho

T

take *v* **(carry)** levar; **(medicine)** tomar; **(time)** demorar

take away [BE] para levar

tampons os tampões higiênicos

taste *v* provar

text *v* **(send a message)** escrever uma mensagem;
n **(message)** mensagem de texto

thank you obrigado m; obrigada f

thirsty com sede

this este, esta

ticket o bilhete; ~ **machine** a máquina de venda de bilhetes;
~ **office** a bilheteria

tired cansado, cansada

today hoje

together juntos

toilet a casa de banho

toilet paper o papel higiênico

tomorrow amanhã

tonight hoje à noite; **for** ~ para hoje à noite

too (much) demasiado; **(also)** também

toothbrush a escova de dentes

Mexican
Spanish

Essentials

Hello.	**¡Hola!** *oh-lah*
Goodbye.	**Adiós.** *ah-deeyohs*
Yes.	**Sí.** *see*
No.	**No.** *noh*
OK.	**De acuerdo.** *deh ah-kwehr-doh*
Excuse me! (to get attention)	**¡Disculpe!** *dihs-koohl-peh*
Excuse me. (to get past)	**Perdón.** *pehr-dohn*
I'm sorry.	**Lo siento.** *loh seeyehn-toh*
I'd like…	**Quiero…** *keeyeh-roh*
How much?	**¿Cuánto (es)?** *kwahn-toh (ehs)*
Where is…?	**¿Dónde está…?** *dohn-deh ehs-tah…*
Please.	**Por favor.** *pohr fah-bohr*
Thank you.	**Gracias.** *grah-seeyahs*
You're welcome.	**De nada.** *deh nah-dah*
Please speak slowly.	**Hable más despacio, por favor.** *ah-blahr mahs dehs-pah-seeyoh, pohr fah-bohr*
Can you repeat that?	**¿Podría repetir eso?** *poh-dree-ah rreh-peh-teer eh-soh*
I don't understand.	**No entiendo.** *noh ehn-teeyehn-doh*
Do you speak English?	**¿Habla inglés?** *ah-blah een-glehs*
I don't speak Spanish.	**No hablo español.** *noh ah-bloh ehs-pah-nyol*
Where's the restroom [toilet]?	**¿Dónde está el baño?** *dohn-deh ehs-tah ehl bah-noh*
Help!	**¡Auxilio!** *aw-xee-leeyoh*

Numbers

0	**cero**	seh·roh
1	**uno**	oo·noh
2	**dos**	dohs
3	**tres**	trehs
4	**cuatro**	kwah·troh
5	**cinco**	seen·koh
6	**seis**	seyees
7	**siete**	seeyeh·teh
8	**ocho**	oh·choh
9	**nueve**	nweh·beh
10	**diez**	deeyehs
11	**once**	ohn·seh
12	**doce**	doh·seh
13	**trece**	treh·seh
14	**catorce**	kah·tohr·seh
15	**quince**	keen·seh
16	**dieciséis**	deeyeh·see·seyees
17	**diecisiete**	deeyeh·see·seeyeh·teh
18	**dieciocho**	deeyeh·see·oh·choh
19	**diecinueve**	deeyeh·see·nweh·beh
20	**veinte**	beyeen·teh

You'll find the pronunciation of the Mexican Spanish letters and words written in gray after each sentence to guide you. Simply pronounce these as if they were English. As you hear the language being spoken, you will quickly become accustomed to the local pronunciation and dialect.

21	**veintiuno** *beyeen·tee·oo·noh*	
22	**veintidós** *beyeen·tee·dohs*	
30	**treinta** *treyeen·tah*	
31	**treinta y uno** *treyeen·tah ee oo·noh*	
40	**cuarenta** *kwah·rehn·tah*	
50	**cincuenta** *seen·kwehn·tah*	
60	**sesenta** *seh·sehn·tah*	
70	**setenta** *seh·tehn·tah*	
80	**ochenta** *oh·chehn·tah*	
90	**noventa** *noh·behn·tah*	
100	**cien** *seeyehn*	
101	**ciento uno** *seeyehn·toh oo·noh*	
200	**doscientos** *dohs·seeyehn·tohs*	
500	**quinientos** *kee·neeyehn·tohs*	
1,000	**mil** *meel*	
10,000	**diez mil** *deeyehs meel*	
1,000,000	**un millón** *oon mee·yohn*	

Time

What time is it?	**¿Qué hora es?** *keh oh·rah ehs*
It's midday.	**Son las doce del día.** *sohn lahs doh·seh dehl dee·ah*

In Mexico you use the greeting **Buenos días** until lunch time (about 2:00p.m.). After 2:00p.m., you should use **Buenos tardes** (good afternoon/evening) up until it gets dark. **Buenas noches** is then used. It also means good night.

70

At midnight.	**A medianoche.** *ah meh•deeyah•noh•cheh*
From one o'clock to two o'clock.	**De una a dos en punto.** *deh oo•nah ah dohs ehn poon•toh*
Five past three.	**Las tres y cinco.** *lahs trehs ee seen•koh*
A quarter to five.	**Cuarto para las cinco.** *kwahr•toh pah•rah lahs seen•koh*
5:30 a.m./p.m.	**Las cinco y media de la mañana/tarde.** *lahs seen•koh ee meh•deeyah deh lah mah•nyah•nah/ tahr•deh*

Dates follow a day-month-year format in Mexico:
el uno de marzo de 2014 = March 1, 2014 = 1.3.14 = 3/1/2014

Days

Monday	**lunes**	*loo·nehs*
Tuesday	**martes**	*mahr·tehs*
Wednesday	**miércoles**	*meeyehr·koh·lehs*
Thursday	**jueves**	*khweh·behs*
Friday	**viernes**	*beeyehr·nehs*
Saturday	**sábado**	*sah·bah·doh*
Sunday	**domingo**	*doh·meen·goh*

Dates

yesterday	**ayer**	*ah·yehr*
today	**hoy**	*oy*
tomorrow	**mañana**	*mah·nyah·nah*
day	**día**	*dee·ah*
week	**semana**	*seh·mah·nah*
month	**mes**	*mehs*
year	**año**	*ah·nyoh*

Months

January	**enero**	*eh·neh·roh*
February	**febrero**	*feh·breh·roh*
March	**marzo**	*mahr·soh*
April	**abril**	*ah·breel*
May	**mayo**	*mah·yoh*
June	**junio**	*khoo·neeyoh*
July	**julio**	*khoo·leeyoh*
August	**agosto**	*ah·gohs·toh*
September	**septiembre**	*sehp·teeyehm·breh*
October	**octubre**	*ohk·too·breh*
November	**noviembre**	*noh·beeyehm·breh*
December	**diciembre**	*dee·seeyehm·breh*

Arrival & Departure

I'm here on vacation [holiday]/business. **Estoy aquí de vacaciones/en viaje de negocios.** *ehs•toy ah•kee deh bah•kah•seeyoh•nehs/ehn beeyah•kheh deh neh•goh•seeyohs*

I'm going to... **Voy a...** *boy ah...*

I'm staying at the...Hotel. **Me alojo en el Hotel...** *meh ah•loh•khoh ehn ehl oh•tehl...*

Money

Where's...? **¿Dónde está...?** *dohn•deh ehs•tah...*

the ATM **el cajero automático** *ehl kah•kheh•roh aw•toh•mah•tee•koh*

the bank **el banco** *ehl bahn•koh*

Instructions on **ATM machines** are usually given in Spanish. However, those located at international airports and major tourist destinations will most likely have English-language instructions and may even dispense U.S. dollars. Note that while debit cards are readily accepted in most places, many convenience stores may only accept cash. The best rates for exchanging money are usually the banks.

YOU MAY SEE…

INTRODUCIR TARJETA AQUÍ	insert card here
CANCELAR	cancel
BORRAR	clear
INTRODUCIR	enter
NIP	PIN
RETIRAR FONDOS	withdraw
DE CUENTA DE CHEQUES	from checking [current] account
DE CUENTA DE AHORROS	from savings account
COMPROBANTE	receipt

the currency exchange office	**la casa de cambio** lah kah·sah deh kahm·beeyoh
When does the bank open/close?	**¿A qué hora abre/cierra el banco?** ah keh oh·rah ah·breh/seeyeh·rrah ehl bahn·koh
I'd like to change some dollars/pounds into pesos.	**Quiero cambiar dólares/libras a pesos.** keeyeh·roh kahm·beeyahr doh·lah·rehs/lee·brahs ah peh·sohs
I want to cash some traveler's checks [cheques].	**Quiero cobrar cheques de viajero.** keeyeh·roh koh·brahr cheh·kehs deh beeyah·kheh·roh

For Numbers, see page 68.

Getting Around

How do I get to town?	**¿Cómo se llega a la ciudad?** koh·moh seh yeh·gah ah lah seew·dahd
Where's…?	**¿Dónde está…?** dohn·deh ehs·tah…
the airport	**el aeropuerto** ehl ah·eh·roh·pwehr·toh
the train station	**la estación del tren** lah ehs·tah·seeyohn dehl trehn

73

YOU MAY HEAR...

Derecho/recto *deh·reh·choh/rrehk·toh*　　　straight ahead

a la izquierda *ah lah ees·keeyehr·dah*　　　left

a la derecha *ah lah deh·reh·chah*　　　right

en/doblando la esquinaehn/　　　around the corner
doh·blahn·doh lah ehs·kee·nah

frente a *frehn·teh ah*　　　opposite

detrás de *deh·trahs deh*　　　behind

al lado de *ahl lah·doh deh*　　　next to

después de *dehs·pwehs deh*　　　after

al norte/sur *ahl nohr·teh/soor*　　　north/south

al este/oeste *ahl ehs·teh/oh·ehs·teh*　　　east/west

en el semáforo *en ehl seh·mah·foh·roh*　　　at the traffic light

en el cruce en *ehl kroo·seh*　　　at the intersection

the bus station	**la estación de camiones** *lah ehs·tah·seeyohn deh kah·meeyoh·nehs*
the subway [underground]	**la estación del metro** *lah ehs·tah·seeyohn*
How far is it?	**¿A qué distancia está?** *ah keh dees·tahn·seeyah ehs·tah*
Where do I buy a ticket?	**¿Dónde puedo comprar el boleto?** *dohn·deh pweh·doh kohm·prahr ehl*
A one-way/return-trip ticket to...	**Un boleto sencillo/redondo a...** *oon boh·leh·toh sehn·see·yoh/rreh·dohn·doh ah...*
How much?	**¿Cuánto es?** *kwahn·toh ehs*
Which gate/line/platform?	**¿Cuál puerta de embarque/línea andén?** *kwahl pwehr·tah deh ehm·bahr·keh/lee·neh·ah/ ahn·dehn*

Where can I get a taxi?	**¿Dónde puedo tomar un taxi?** *dohn·deh pweh·doh toh·mahr oon tah·xee*	Essentials
Take me to this address.	**Lléveme a esta dirección.** *yeh·beh·meh ah ehs·tah dee·rehk·seeyohn*	
Where's the car rental [hire]?	**¿Dónde está la renta de autos?** *dohn·deh ehs·ta lah rrehn·tah deh aw·tohs*	
Can I have a map?	**¿Puede darme un mapa?** *pweh·deh dahr·meh oon mah·pah*	

Tickets

75

When's…to Acapulco?	**¿Cuándo sale…a Acapulco?** *kwahn·doh sah·leh…ah ah·kah·pool·koh*	
the (first) bus	**el (primer) camión** *ehl (pree·mehr) kah·meeyohn*	
the (next) flight	**el (siguiente) vuelo** *ehl (see·geeyehn·teh) bweh·loh*	
the (last) train	**el (último) tren** *ehl (ool·tee·moh) trehn*	

Mexico has very limited passenger rail service. Instead, a plethora of private intercity bus lines serve this nation. The **Chihuahua Pacific Express (Chepe)** is a notable exception, an engineering feat and a 630 km spectacular trip.

Where do I buy a ticket?	**¿Dónde puedo comprar el boleto?** *dohn•deh pweh•doh kohm•prahr ehl boh•leh•toh*
One/Two ticket(s) please.	**Un/Dos boleto(s), por favor.** *oon/dohs boh•leh•toh(s) pohr fah•bohr*
For today/tomorrow.	**Para hoy/mañana.** *pah•rah oy/mah•nyah•nah*
A . . . ticket.	**Un boleto. . .** *oon boh•leh•toh. . .*
one-way	**sencillo** *sehn•see•yoh*
return trip	**redondo** *rreh•dohn•doh*
first class	**de primera clase** *deh pree•meh•rah klah•seh*
business class	**de clase ejecutiva** *deh klah•seh ehe•ku•ti•vah*
economy class	**clase turista** *klah•seh tuh•rees•tah*
How much?	**¿Cuánto es?** *kwahn•toh ehs*

YOU MAY SEE...

ANDENES	platforms
INFORMACIÓN	information
RESERVACIONES	reservations
SALA DE ESPERA	waiting room
LLEGADAS	arrivals
SALIDAS	departures

The bus service in Mexico is extensive. For local service within a town or city, you pay as you board the bus. The fare depends on the distance you travel. Buses are known by different names: **camión, micro, pesera.** The **camión** is the public bus. **Micro** and **pesera** are privately operated; the **micro** is larger than the **pesera**, but not as large as the **camión.**

Is there a discount for...?	**¿Hacen descuento a...?** *ah·sehn dehs·kwehn·toh ah...*	
children	**niños** *nee·nyohs*	
students	**estudiantes** *ehs·too·deeyahn·tehs*	
senior citizens	**personas de la tercera edad** *pehr·soh·nahs deh lah ltehr·seh·rah eh·dahd*	
tourists	**turistas** *too·ris·tahs*	
The express bus/ express train, please.	**El camión/tren express, por favor** *Ehl kah·meeyon/ trehn express por fah·vohr*	
The local bus/train, please.	**El camion/tren local, por favor** *Ehl kah·meeyon/ trehn lo·kahl por fah·vohr*	

YOU MAY HEAR...

Boletos, por favor.
boh·leh·tohs pohr fah·bohr

Tickets, please.

Tiene que transbordar en...
teeyeh·neh keh trahnz·bohr·dahr ehn...

You have to change at...

Próxima parada: Chihuahua.
proh·xee·mah pah·rah·dah chee·wah·wah

Next stop... Chihuahua.

PARADA DE CAMIONES	bus stop
PEDIR PARADA	request stop
SUBIR/BAJAR	entrance/exit
MARQUE SU BOLETO	stamp your ticket

I have an e-ticket.   **Tengo un boleto electrónico** *tehn•go oon boh•leh•toh electroh•nikoh*

Can I buy...   **¿Puedo comprar ...?** *pweh•doh kohm•prahr ...*

  a ticket on the bus/train?   **el boleto a bordo del camión/ tren** *ehl boh•leh•toh ah bohr•doh dehl kah•meeyohn/ trehn*

  the ticket before boarding?   **el boleto antes de abordar** *ehl boh•leh•toh ahn•tehs deh abohr•dahr*

How long is this ticket valid?   **¿Por cuánto tiempo es válido el boleto?** *Pohr cuahn•to tyehm•poh ehs vah•lidoh ehl boh•leh•toh?*

Can I return on the same ticket?   **¿Puedo volver con el mismo boleto?** *Pueh•doh vol•vehr con ehl mees•moh boh•leh•toh?*

I'd like to...   **Quiero...mi reservación** *kyeh•roh... mee rreh•sehr•vah•ceeohn*

my reservation.

  cancel   **cancelar** *cahn•ceh•lahr*

  change   **cambiar** *cahm•bee•ahr*

  confirm   **confirmar** *cohn•feer•mahr*

For Time, see page 69.

Car Hire

Where's the car hire?   **¿Dónde puedo rentar un auto?** *dohn•deh pweh•doh rrehn•tahr oon aw•toh*

I'd like...   **Quiero...** *keeyeh•roh...*

  a cheap/small car   **un auto barato/compacto** *oonaw•toh bah•rah•toh/ kohm•pahk•toh*

an automatic/ a manual	**un auto automático/manual** *oon autto autto·mah·teeco/mahn·uahl*
air conditioning	**un auto con aire acondicionado** *oon aw·toh kohn* *ayee·reh ah·kohn·dee·seeyoh·nah·doh*
a car seat	**un asiento de niño** *oon ah·seeyehn·toh deh nee·nyoh*
How much…?	**¿Cuánto cobran…?** *kwahn·toh koh·brahn…*

YOU MAY HEAR…

¿Tiene licencia de conducir international?
teeyeh·neh lee·sehn·seeyah deh kohn·doo·seer
een·tehr·nah·seeyoh·nahl

Do you have an
international driver's
license?

Su pasaporte, por favor.
soo pah·sah·pohr·teh pohr fah·bohr

Your passport, please.

¿Quiere seguro?
keeyeh·reh seh·goo·roh

Do you want insurance?

Necesitaré un depósito.
neh·seh·see·tah·reh oon deh·poh·see·toh

I'll need a deposit.

Ponga sus iniciales/Firme aquí.
Pohn·gah soos eenee·syah·lehs/Feer·meh ah·kee

Initial/Sign here.

YOU MAY SEE...

EMPUJAR/JALAR	push/pull
BAÑO/SANITARIOS	bathroom [toilet]
REGADERA	shower
ELEVADOR	elevator [lift]
ESCALERAS	stairs
MÁQUINAS DISPENSADORAS	vending machines
HIELO	ice
LAVANDERÍA	laundry
NO MOLESTAR	do not disturb
PUERTA DE INCENDIOS	fire door
SALIDA (DE EMERGENCIA)	(emergency) exit
SERVICIO DE DESPERTADOR	wake-up call

Communications

Where's an internet cafe?	**¿Dónde hay un café Internet?** *dohn·deh aye oon cah·feh een·tehr·neht*
Can I access the internet/check email?	**¿Puedo entrar a Internet/revisar el correo electrónico?** *pweh·doh ehn·trahrah een·tehr·neht/ reh·bee·sahr ehl koh·rreh·oh eh·lehk·troh·nee·koh*
How much per (half) hour?	**¿Cuánto cuesta por (media) hora?** *kwan·toh kwehs·tah pohr (meh·deeyah) oh·rah*
How do I connect/ log on?	**¿Cómo me conecto/inicio la sesión?** *koh·moh meh koh·nehk·toh/ee·nee·seeyoh lah seh·seeyohn*
A phone card, please.	**Una tarjeta de teléfono, por favor.** *oo·nah tahr·kheh·tah deh teh·leh·foh·noh pohr fah·bohr*
Can I have your phone number?	**¿Me puede dar su número de teléfono?** *meh pweh·deh dahr soo noo·meh·roh deh teh·leh·foh·noh*

Here's my number/ e-mail.	**Este es mi número/Esta es mi dirección de correo electrónico.** *ehs·teh ehs mee noo·meh·roh/ehs·tah ehs mee dee·rehk·seeyohn deh koh·rreh·oh eh·lehk·troh·nee·koh*
Call me.	**Llámeme.** *yah·meh·meh*
E-mail me.	**Envíeme un correo electrónico.** *ehn·bee·eh·meh oon koh·rreh·oh eh·lehk·troh·nee·koh*
Hello. This is…	**Hola. Soy…** *oh·lah soy…*
Can I speak to…?	**¿Puedo hablar con…?** *pweh·doh ah·blahr kohn…*
Can you repeat that?	**¿Puede repetir eso?** *pweh·deh rreh·peh·teer eh·soh*
I'll call back later.	**Llamaré más tarde.** *yah·mah·reh mahs tahr·deh*
Bye.	**Adiós.** *ah·deeyohs*
Where's the post office?	**¿Dónde está la oficina de correos?** *dohn·deh ehs·tah lah oh·fee·see·nah deh koh·rreh·ohs*
I'd like to send this to…	**Quiero mandar esto a…** *keeyeh·roh mahn·dahr ehs·toh ah…*

There are many **internet cafes** throughout Mexico, especially in bigger cities. These are very popular, as not everyone has personal access to the internet. You usually pay a set fee per hour.

Public phones in Mexico are coin or card operated, but they are a rare sight these days. Phone cards can be purchased at newsstands and supermarkets. There is good cell phone coverage in most of the country; **GSM** is the most widely used system. For international calls, prepaid calling cards are the most economical option and are available at most newsstands. You can also make long-distance calls at **centros de negocios** (business centers). The latter also offer internet, fax and wireless phone-charging services at reasonable prices.

Social Media

Are you on Facebook/ Twitter?	**¿Estás en Facebook/Twitter?** *Ehs·tahs ehn Facebook/ Twitter?*
What's your user name?	**¿Cuál es tu nombre de usuario?** *Kwahl ehs too nohm·breh deh u·swah·ryoh?*
I'll add you as a friend.	**Te añadiré como amigo.** *Teh a·nyah·dee·reh co·moh amee·go*
I'll follow you on Twitter.	**Te seguiré en Twitter.** *Te seh·guee·reh ehn Twitter*

YOU MAY SEE...

CERRAR	close
BORRAR	delete
CORREO ELECTRÓNICO	email
SALIR	exit
AYUDA	help
MENSAJERO INSTANTÁNEO	instant messenger
INTERNET	internet
INICIAR SESIÓN	log in
NUEVO (MENSAJE)	new (message)
PRENDER/APAGAR	on/off
ABRIR	open
IMPRIMIR	print
GUARDAR	save
ENVIAR	send
NOMBRE DE USUARIO/CONTRASEÑA	username/password
INTERNET INALÁMBRICO	wireless internet

Are you following...? **¿Estás siguiendo a...?** *ehs·tahs see·ghee-ehn·do ah*

I'll put the pictures on Facebook/Twitter. **Pondré las fotos en Facebook/Twitter** *Pond·reh lahs foh·tohs ehn Facebook/Twittter*

I'll tag you in the pictures. **Te etiquetaré en las fotos.** *Teh ehti·ketah·reh ehn lahs foh·tohs*

Conversation

Hello!/Hi!	**¡Hola!** *oh·lah*
How are you?	**¿Cómo estás?** *koh·moh ehs·tahs*
Fine, thanks.	**Bien, gracias.** *beeyehn grah·seeyahs*
Excuse me!	**¡Disculpe!** *dihs·koohl·peh*
Do you speak English?	**¿Habla inglés?** *ah·blah een·glehs*

YOU MAY HEAR...

Hablo muy poco inglés.
ah·bloh mooy poh·koh een·glehs

No hablo inglés
ah·bloh een·glehs

I only speak a little
English.

I don't speak English.

What's your name?	**¿Cómo se llama?** *koh·moh seh yah·mah*
My name is...	**Me llamo...** *meh yah·moh...*
Nice to meet you.	**Encantado m/Encantada f.** *ehn·kahn·tah·doh/ ehn·kahn·tah·dah*
Where are you from?	**¿De dónde es usted?** *deh dohn·deh es oos·tehd*
I'm from the U.K./U.S.	**Soy de Estados Unidos/del Reino Unido.** *soy deh ehs·tah·dohs oo·nee·dohs/dehl rreeyee·noh oo·nee·doh*
What do you do for a living?	**¿A qué se dedica?** *ah keh seh deh·dee·kah*
I work for...	**Trabajo para...** *trah·bah·khoh pah·rah...*
I'm a student.	**Soy estudiante.** *soy ehs·too·deeyahn·teh*

When meeting someone for the first time in Mexico greet him or her with **hola** (hello), **buenos días** (good morning), **buenas tardes** (good afternoon) or **buenas noches** (good evening). Mexicans even extend this general greeting to strangers when in elevators, waiting rooms and other small public spaces. A general acknowledgment or reply is expected from all. When leaving, say **adiós** (goodbye).

I'm retired.	**Estoy jubilado *m*/jubilada *f*.** *ehs·toy khoo·bee·lah·doh/khoo·bee·lah·dah*
Do you like…?	**¿Le gusta…?** *leh goos·tah…*
Goodbye.	**Adiós.** *ah·deeyohs*
See you later.	**Hasta luego.** *ah·stah lweh·goh*

Romance

Would you like to go out for a drink/dinner?	**¿Le gustaría salir a tomar una copa/cenar?** *leh goos·tah·ree·ah sah·leer ah toh·mahr oo·nah koh·pah/seh·nahr*
What are your plans for tonight/tomorrow?	**¿Qué planes tiene para esta noche/mañana?** *keh plah·nehs teeyeh·neh pah·rah ehs·tah noh·cheh/mah·nyah·nah*
Can I have your (phone) number?	**¿Puede darme su número?** *pweh·deh dahr·meh soo noo·meh·roh*
Can I join you?	**¿Puedo acompañarlo *m*/acompañarla *f*?** *ah·kohm·pah·nyahr·loh/ah·kohm·pah·nyahr·lah*
Can I buy you a drink?	**¿Puedo invitarle una copa?** *pweh·doh een·bee·tahr·leh oo·nah koh·pah*
I love you.	**Te amo.** *teh ah·moh*

Accepting & Rejecting

I'd love to.	**Me encantaría.**
	meh ehn•kahn•tah•ree•yah
Where should we meet?	**¿Dónde nos vemos?**
	dohn•deh nohs beh•mohs
I'll meet you at the bar/your hotel.	**Nos vemos en el bar/tu hotel.**
	nohs beh•mohs ehn ehl bahr/too oh•tehl
I'll come by at…	**Pasaré a…**
	pah•sah•reh ah…
I'm busy.	**Estoy ocupado *m*/ocupada *f*.**
	ehs•toy oh•koo•pah•doh/oh•koo•pah•dah
I'm not interested.	**No me interesa.** *noh meh een•teh•reh•sah*
Leave me alone.	**Déjeme en paz.** *deh•kheh•meh ehn pahs*
Stop bothering me!	**¡Deje de molestarme!**
	deh•kheh deh moh•lehs•tahr•meh

For Time, see page 69.

Food & Drink

Eating Out

Can you recommend a good restaurant/bar?	**¿Puede recomendarme un buen restaurante/bar?** *pweh•deh rreh•koh•mehn•dahr•meh oon bwehn rrehs•taw•rahn•teh/bahr*
Is there a traditional /an inexpensive restaurant nearby?	**¿Hay un restaurante típico/barato cerca de aquí?** *aye oon rrehs•taw•rahn•teh tee•pee•koh/ bah•rah•toh sehr•kah deh ah•kee*
A table for…, please.	**Una mesa para…, por favor.** *oo•nah meh•sah pah•rah…pohr fah•bohr*
Can we sit…?	**¿Podemos sentarnos…?** *poh•deh•mohs sehn•tahr•nohs…*
here/there	**aquí/allá** *ah•kee/ah•yah*
outside	**afuera** *ah•fweh•rah*
in a non-smoking area	**en el área de no fumar** *ehn ehl ah•reh•ah deh noh foo•mahr*
I'm waiting for someone.	**Estoy esperando a alguien.** *ehs•toy ehs•peh•rahn•doh ah ahl•geeyehn*
Where are the toilets?	**¿Dónde está el baño?** *dohn•deh ehs•tah ehl bah•nyo*

The menu, please.	**Un menú, por favor.** *oon meh·noo pohr fah·bohr*
What do you recommend?	**¿Qué me recomienda?** *keh meh rreh·koh·meeyehn·dah*
I'd like…	**Quiero…** *keeyeh·roh…*
Some more…, please.	**Quiero más…, por favor.** *keeyeh·roh mahs… pohr fah·bohr*
Enjoy your meal!	**¡Buen provecho!** *bwen proh·beh·choh*
The check [bill], please.	**La cuenta, por favor.** *lah kwen·tah pohr fah·bohr*
Is service included?	**¿Está incluido el cubierto?** *ehs·tah een·kloo·ee·doh ehl koo·beeyehr·toh*
Can I pay by credit card?	**¿Puedo pagar con tarjeta de crédito?** *pweh·dohpah·gahr kohn tahr·kheh·tah deh kreh·dee·toh*
Can I have a receipt?	**¿Podría darme un comprobante?** *poh·dree·ah dahr·meh oon kohm·proh·bahn·teh*

Breakfast

tocino *toh·cee·noh*	bacon
el pan *ehl pahn*	bread
la mantequilla *lah mahn·teh·kee·yah*	butter
las carnes frías *lahs kahr·nehs free·ahs*	cold cuts
el queso *ehl keh·soh*	cheese

el huevo... *ehl weh·boh...*	...egg
duro/tibio *doo·roh/tee·beeyoh*	hard/soft boiled
frito *free·toh*	fried
revuelto *rreh·bwehl·toh*	scrambled
la mermelada/la jalea	jam/jelly
lah mehr·meh·lah·dah/khah·leh·ah	
el omelet... *ehl oh·meh·leht...*	omelet
el pan tostado *ehl pahn tohs·tah·doh*	toast
la salchicha *lah sahl·chee·chah*	sausage
el yogur *ehl yoh·goor*	yogurt

Appetizers

las chalupas *lahs chah·loo·pahs*	tortillas with potato, chicken, onion and salsa topping
el chicharrón *ehl chee·chah·rrohn*	deep fried pork skin
los frijoles refritos	mashed and fried
lohs free·khoh·lehs rreh·free·tohs	black beans
las gorditas *lahs gohr·dee·tahs*	little corn cakes baked or fried
el guacamole *ehl gwa·hkah·moh·leh*	mashed avocado, onions, tomatoes and lime juice

las quesadillas *lahs keh•sah•dee•yahs* — corn tortillas stuffed with cheese, beef, chicken, etc.

el queso fundido *ehl keh•soh foon•dee•doh* — Mexican fondue

la salsa *lah sahl•sah* — chopped or pureed tomatoes, chiles, onions and cilantro

los tacos *lohs tah•kohs* — soft tortillas filled with a variety of meat and vegetables

la tortilla *lah tohr•tee•yah* — thin, flat bread made of corn

Meat

la carne de res *lah kahr•neh deh rehs*	beef
el pollo *ehl poh•yoh*	chicken
el cordero *ehl kohr•deh•roh*	lamb
la carne de puerco *lah kahr•neh deh pwehr•koh*	pork
el filete *ehl fee•leh•teh*	steak
la ternera *lah tehr•neh•rah*	veal

Fish & Seafood

las almejas *lahs ahl•meh•khahs*	clam
el bacalao *ehl bah•kah•la•oh*	cod
el cangrejo *ehl kahn•greh•khoh*	crab

el acocil *ehl ah•koh•seel* crayfish
la merluza *lah mehr•loo•sah* hake
el arenque *ehl ah•rehn•keh* herring
la langosta *lah lahn•gohs•tah* lobster
la sierra *lah see•eh•rrah* mackerel
los mejillones *lohs meh•khee•yoh•nehs* mussels

Meat dishes are popular in Mexico, and the northern states of **Sonora** and **Chihuahua** are famous for their cuts of beef. Traditional dishes include **carne asada** (grilled meat), which is usually served with a side of tortillas, beans, grilled onions and salsa. Another Mexican specialty is the **barbacoa:** mutton cooked in the ground with spices and wrapped in maguey leaves. The resulting broth is seasoned and served as a soup.

The **torta**, which is basically a sandwich made with a kind of white bread, is also a specialty. These are filled with **frijoles refritos** (mashed and fried black beans), meat, lettuce, tomato, onion and chili, among other things. They can have many ingredients or just a few, depending on each person's taste.

el pulpo *ehl pool•poh*		octopus
el ostión *lah ohs•tee•ohn*		oyster
los langostinos *lohs lahn•gohs•tee•nohs*		prawns
el salmón *ehl sahl•mohn*		salmon
el tiburón *ehl tee•boo•rohn*		shark
el lenguado *ehl lehn•gwah•doh*		sole
el pez espada *ehl pehs ehs•pah•dah*		swordfish

Ceviche is a dish made by marinating raw fish with lime.
The lime adds flavor and cooks the fish without using heat. The
preparation includes chopped onions, tomato and olives, with a dash
of hot salsa. **Ceviche** is served cold, accompanied by crackers.

ceviche... *seh•bee•cheh...*	marinated, raw...
de callos de hacha *deh kah•yohs deh ah•chah*	scallops
de camarones *deh kah•mah•roh•nehs*	shrimp
de langostinos *deh lahn•gohs•tee•nohs*	prawn
de mariscos *deh mah•rees•kohs*	mixed seafood
de pescado *deh pehs•kah•do*	fish
de pulpo *deh pool•poh*	octopus

la trucha *lah troo•chah*	trout
el atún *ehl ah•toon*	tuna

Vegetables

el aguacate *ehl ah•gwah•khah•teh*	avocado
los frijoles *lah free•kho•lehs*	beans
el germen de soya *ehl gehr•mehn deh soh•yah*	bean sprouts
las habas *lahs ah•bahs*	broad beans
el ejote *ehl eh•khoh•teh*	green bean
la col *lah kohl*	cabbage
el champiñón *ehl chahm•pee•nyohn*	mushroom
la cebolla *lah seh•boh•yah*	onion
el chícharo *ehl chee•chah•roh*	green pea
el chile *ehl chee•leh*	hot pepper
el chile chipotle *ehl chee•leh chee•poh•tleh*	chipotle pepper
el chile jalapeño *ehl chee•leh khah•lah•peh•nyo*	jalapeño pepper
el chile verde *ehl chee•leh behr•deh*	hot green pepper
la papa *lah pah•pah*	potato
el jitomate *ehl khee•toh•mah•teh*	tomato

What do you recommend?	**¿Qué me recomienda?** *keh meh rreh•koh•meeyehn•dah*
I'd like a bottle/glass of red/white wine.	**Quiero una botella/una copa de vino tinto/blanco.** *keeyeh•roh oo•nah boh•teh•yah/oo•nah koh•pah deh bee•noh teen•toh/blahn•koh*
The house wine, please.	**El vino de la casa, por favor.** *ehl bee•noh deh lah kah•sah pohr fah•bohr*

There are many popular brands of Mexican beer, such as **Corona®**, **Sol®**, **Tecate®** and **Victoria®**, to name a few. Each brand usually has several classes and types of beer available, though most will be a lager-type beer.

Mexican wine is produced in the northern part of the country, with the **state of Baja California** being the best producer.

Wine routes can be followed in northern Mexico – about 50 wineries, from small family-owned to mass producers, can be visited. Tours of the winery and vineyards may be available and some may have on-site restaurants and shops.

Many Mexicans love coffee and drink it throughout the day. **Café de olla** is coffee prepared in a clay pot, sweetened with **piloncillo** (brown sugar). **Café lechero** is coffee mixed with steamed milk. Tap water is not always safe to drink. Restaurants often serve bottled water with meals, unless you specifically request **agua de la llave** (tap water). Juice is usually served with breakfast, but it's not common at lunch or dinner.

Another bottle/glass, please.	**Otra botella/copa, por favor.** *oh·trah boh·teh·yah/koh·pah pohr fah·bohr*
I'd like a local beer.	**Quiero una cerveza nacional.** *keeyeh·roh oo·nah sehr·beh·sah nah·seeoh·nhal*
Can I buy you a drink?	**¿Puedo invitarle una copa?** *pweh·doh een·bee·tahr·leh oo·nah koh·pah*
Cheers!	**¡Salud!** *sah·lood*
A coffee/tea, please.	**Un café/té, por favor.** *oon kah·feh/teh pohr fah·bohr*
Black.	**Solo.** *soh·loh*
With...	**Con...** *kohn...*
milk	**leche** *leh·cheh*
sugar	**azúcar** *ah·soo·kahr*
artificial sweetener	**endulzante artificial** *ehn·dool·sahn·teh ahr·tee·fee·seeyahl*
A..., please.	**..., por favor.** *...pohr fah·bohr*
juice	**Un jugo** *khoo·goh*
soda	**Un refresco** *rreh·frehs·koh*
(sparkling/still) water	**Un agua (con/sin gas)** *ah·gwah (kohn/seen gahs)*

Leisure Time

Sightseeing

Where's the tourist information office?	**¿Dónde está la oficina de turismo?** *dohn•deh ehs•tah lah oh•fee•see•nah deh too•reez•moh*
What are the main sights?	**¿Dónde están los principales sitios de interés?** *dohn•deh ehs•tahn lohs preen•see•pah•lehs see•teeyohs deh een•teh•rehs*
Do you offer tours in English?	**¿Hay recorridos en inglés?** *aye rreh•koh•rree•dohs ehn een•glehs*
Can I have a map/ guide?	**¿Puede darme un mapa/una guía?** *pweh•deh dahr•meh oon mah•pah/oo•nah gee•ah*

Tourist offices can be found in major Mexican cities and in many of the smaller towns popular with tourists. They generally work regular business hours Monday to Friday and work shorter days on Saturdays and Sundays. Information can also be found via the Mexican Tourism Board's official website **www.visitmexico.com**.

Shopping

Where's the market/mall?	**¿Dónde está el mercado/centro comercial?** *dohn•deh ehs•tah ehl mehr•kah•doh/sen•troh koh•mehr•seeyahl*
I'm just looking.	**Sólo estoy mirando.** *soh•loh ehs•toy mee•rahn•doh*
Can you help me?	**¿Puede ayudarme?** *pweh•deh ah•yoo•dahr•meh*
I'm being helped.	**Ya me atienden.** *yah meh ah•teeyehn•dehn*
How much?	**¿Cuánto es?** *kwahn•toh ehs*
That one, please.	**Ése *m*/Ésa *f*, por favor.** *eh•seh/eh•sah pohr fah•bohr*
That's all.	**Eso es todo.** *eh•soh ehs toh•doh*

YOU MAY SEE...

ABIERTO/CERRADO	open/closed
CERRADO DURANTE EL ALMUERZO	closed for lunch
PROBADOR	fitting room
CAJERO	cashier
SOLO EFECTIVO	cash only
SE ACEPTAN TARJETAS DE CRÉDITO	credit cards accepted
HORARIO DE ATENCIÓN	business hours
SALIDA	exit

Tarjetas de crédito (credit cards) are widely accepted, although you may be asked to show ID when using one. **Tarjetas de débito** (debit cards) are also common. Traveler's checks are not accepted everywhere; have an alternative form of payment available. Cash is the preferred method of payment – some places, such as chain convenience stores, newsstands, tobacconists, flower shops and market or street vendors will only take cash. **Mercados** (markets) and **mercados sobre ruedas** (traveling markets – literally 'markets on wheels') are popular. A wide variety of goods is available at these markets, including fruit and vegetables, antiques, souvenirs, regional items and so on. Your hotel or local tourist office will have information on the markets in your area. Most **mercados** are open daily from early morning until late afternoon; the **mercados sobre ruedas** times vary by location.

Where can I pay?	**¿Dónde se paga?** *dohn·deh seh pah·gah*
I'll pay in cash/by credit card.	**Voy a pagar en efectivo/con tarjeta de crédito.** *boy ah pah·gahr ehn eh·fehk·tee·boh/kohn tahr·kheh·tah deh kreh·dee·toh*
A receipt, please.	**Un comprobante, por favor.** *oon kohm·proh·bahn·teh pohr fah·bohr*

Sport & Leisure

When's the game?	**¿Cuándo empieza el partido?** *kwahn·doh ehm·peeyeh·sah ehl pahr·tee·doh*
Where's...?	**¿Dónde está...?** *dohn·deh ehs·tah...*
the beach	**la playa** *lah plah·yah*
the park	**el parque** *ehl pahr·keh*
the pool	**la alberca** *lah ahl·behr·kah*

Is it safe to swim here?	**¿Es seguro nadar aquí?**
	ehs seh•goo•roh nah•dahr ah•kee
Can I hire clubs?	**¿Puedo rentar palos de golf?**
	pweh•doh rrehn•tahr pah•lohs deh golf
How much per hour/day?	**¿Cuánto cuesta por hora?**
	kwahn•toh kwehs•tah pohr oh•rah
How far is it to…?	**¿A qué distancia está…?**
	ah keh dees•tahn•seeyah ehs•tah…
Show me on the map, please.	**¿Puede indicármelo en el mapa, por favor?**
	pweh•deh een•dee•kahr•meh•loh ehn ehl mah•pah
	pohr fah•bohr

Fútbol (soccer) is the most popular sport in Mexico; most of the major cities in Mexico have their own professional teams with a large fan base. Note that fans are extremely dedicated, so be sure not to insult the team. Other popular sports include **fútbol americano** (American football), **básquetbol** (basketball), **boxeo** (boxing), **los toros** or **la fiesta brava** (bullfighting) and **lucha libre** (freestyle wrestling).

Mexico has many miles of coastline and beaches, boasting some of the most beautiful beaches in the **Caribbean (Cancún, Cozumel, the Mayan Riviera)** and the **Pacific Coast (Huatulco, Ixtapa, Puerto Vallarta)**. If you decide to go for a swim, check the safety flags at each beach. Green flags indicate the water is safe, yellow flags indicate that you should use caution and red flags indicate that the water is unsafe for swimming.

Going Out

What's there to do at night?	**¿Qué se puede hacer en la noche?** *keh seh pweh·deh ah·sehr ehn lah noh·cheh*
Do you have a program of events?	**¿Tiene un programa de eventos?** *teeyeh·neh oon proh·grah·mah deh eh·behn·tohs*
What's playing tonight?	**¿Qué hay en cartelera esta noche?** *keh aye ehn kahr·teh·leh·rah ehs·tah noh·cheh*
Where's…?	**¿Dónde está…?** *dohn·deh ehs·tah…*
the downtown area	**el centro** *ehl sehn·troh*
the bar	**el bar** *ehl bahr*
the dance club	**la discoteca** *lah dees·koh·teh·kah*

Baby Essentials

Do you have…?	**¿Tiene…?** *teeyeh•neh…*
a baby bottle	**un biberón** *oon bee•beh•rohn*
baby food	**comida para bebé** *co•mee•dah pahrah beh•beh*
baby wipes	**toallitas para bebé** *toh•ah•yee•tahs pah•rah beh•beh*
a car seat	**un asiento para niños** *oon ah•seeyehn•toh pah•rah nee•nyohs*
a children's menu/ portion	**un menú/una ración para niños** *oon meh•noo/ oo•nah rrah•seeyohn pah•rah nee•nyohs*
a child's seat/ highchair	**una silla para niños/periquera** *oo•nah see•yah pah•rah nee•nyohs/peh•ree•khe•rah*
a crib/cot	**una cuna/un catre** *oo•nah koo•nah/oon kah•treh*
diapers [nappies]	**pañales** *pah•nyah•lehs*
formula	**fórmula** *fohr•moo•lah*
a pacifier [dummy]	**un chupón** *oon choo•pohn*
a playpen	**un corral** *oon koh•rrahl*
a stroller [pushchair]	**una carriola** *oo•nah kah•rreeyoh•lah*
Can I breastfeed the baby here?	**¿Puedo darle pecho al bebé aquí?** *pweh•doh dahr•leh peh•choh ahl beh•beh ah•kee*
Where can I breastfeed/ change the baby?	**¿Dónde puedo cambiar al bebé?** *dohn•deh pweh•doh kahm•beeyahr ahl beh•beh*

Disabled Travelers

Is there…?	**¿Hay…?** *aye…*
access for the disabled	**acceso para los discapacitados** *ahk•seh•soh pah•rah lohs dees•kah•pah•see•tah•dohs*
a wheelchair ramp	**una rampa para sillas de ruedas** *oo•nah rrahm•pah pah•rah see•yahs deh rrweh•dahs*
a disabled-accessible toilet	**un baño con acceso para discapacitados** *oon bah•nyoh kohn ahk•seh•soh pah•rah dees•kah•pah•see•tah•dohs*
I need…	**Necesito…** *neh•seh•see•toh…*
assistance	**ayuda** *ah•yoo•dah*
an elevator [a lift]	**un elevador** *oon eh•leh•bah•dohr*
a ground-floor room	**una habitación en la planta baja** *oo•nah ah•bee•tah•seeyohn ehn lah plahn•tah*

Health & Emergencies

Emergencies

Help!	**¡Auxilio!** *aw·xee·leeyoh*
Go away!	**¡Váyase!** *bah·yah·seh*
Stop, thief!	**¡Alto, ladrón!** *ahl·toh lah·drohn*
Get a doctor!	**¡Llame a un doctor!** *yah·meh ah oon dohk·tohr*

YOU MAY HEAR...

Llene este formulario
yeh·neh ehs·teh fohr·mooh·lah·reeoh

Fill out this form.

Su identificación, por favor.
soo ee·dehn·tee·fee·kah·seeyohn pohr fah·bohr

Your ID, please.

¿Cuándo/Dónde ocurrió?
? kwahn·doh/dohn·deh oh·koo·rreeyoh

When/Where did it happen?

¿Puede describirlo m/describirla f?
? pweh·deh dehs·kree·beer·loh m/ dehs·kree·beer·lah f

What does he/she look like?

Fire! **¡Fuego!** *fweh-goh*

I'm lost. **Me perdí.** *meh pehr-dee*

Can you help me? **¿Puede ayudarme?** *pweh-deh ah-yoo-dahr-meh*

Health

I'm sick. **Me siento mal.** *meh seeyehn-toh mahl*

I need an English-
speaking doctor
Necesito un doctor que hable inglés.
neh-seh-see-toh oon dohk-tohr keh ah-bleh een-glehs

It hurts here. **Me duele aquí.** *meh dweh-leh ah-kee*

Where's the
pharmacy?
¿Dónde está la farmacia? *dohn-deh ehs-tah lah fahr-mah-seeyah*

I'm (...months)
pregnant.
Tengo (...meses) de embarazo.
Tehn-goh (...meh-sehs) deh ehm-bah-rah-soh

I'm on... **Estoy tomando...** *ehs-toy toh-mahn-doh...*

I'm allergic to
antibiotics/penicillin.
**Soy alérgico *m*/alérgica *f* a los antibióticos/
la penicilina.** *soy ah-lehr-khee-koh/
ah-lehr-khee-kah ah lohs ahn-tee-beeyoh-tee-kohs/
lah peh-nee-see-lee-nah*

The emergency number in Mexico varies depending on the
state you are in so it is best to check this on arrival. For the police
and emergency services, **dial 060 (Mexico City and many other
states).** In some parts of Mexico, you will need to **dial 066 (Yucatán).**

Dictionary

A

abbey la abadía
accept *v* aceptar
access el acceso
accident el accidente
accommodation el alojamiento
account la cuenta
acupuncture la acupuntura
adapter el adaptador
address la dirección
admission la entrada
after después; ~ **noon** la tarde; ~ **shave** la loción para después de afeitar
age la edad
agency la agencia
AIDS el sida
air el aire; ~ **conditioning** el aire acondicionado; ~ **line** la aerolínea; ~ **mail** el correo aéreo; ~ **plane** el avión; ~ **port** el aeropuerto
aisle el pasillo; ~ **seat** el asiento de pasillo
allergic alérgico; ~ **reaction** la reacción alérgica
allow *v* permitir
alone solo
alter *v* **(clothing)** hacer un ajuste
alternate route el otro camino
aluminum foil el papel aluminio
amazing increíble
ambulance la ambulancia
American estadounidense
appointment la cita
attractive guapo

Australia Australia
Australian australiano
automatic automático; ~ **car** auto automático
available disponible

B

baby el bebé; ~ **bottle** el biberón; ~ **wipe** la toallita; ~ **sitter** la niñera
back la espalda; ~ **ache** el dolor de espalda; ~ **pack** la mochila
bag la maleta
baggage el equipaje; ~ **claim** el reclamo de equipaje; ~ **ticket** el talón de equipaje
bakery la panadería
barbecue la parrillada
barber la peluquería
bathroom el baño
beach la playa
beautiful bello
beginner principiante
best mejor
better mejor
bicycle la bicicleta
big grande
bigger más grande
bike route la ruta para bicicletas
bikini el bikini; ~ **wax** la depilación de las ingles
bill *v* **(charge)** cobrar; ~ *n* **(money)** el billete; ~ *n* **(of sale)** el recibo
bird el pájaro
black negro
bland insípido
boarding pass el pase de abordar
boat el barco

book el libro; **~store** la librería

bottle la botella; **~ opener** el destapador

boy el niño; **~ friend** el novio

break *v* romper

break-in (burglary) el allanamiento de morada

breakdown la avería

breakfast el desayuno

British británico

brother el hermano

bus el camión; **~ station** la estación de camiones; **~ stop** la parada de camiones; **~ ticket** el boleto del camión; **~ tour** el recorrido en camión

business los negocios; **~ card** la tarjeta de presentación; **~ center** el centro de negocios; **~ class** la clase ejecutiva; **~ hours** el horario de atención al público

C

call *v* llamar; **~***n* la llamada

can opener el abrelatas

car el auto; **~ hire [BE]** la renta de autos; **~ park [BE]** el estacionamiento; **~ rental** el alquiler de autos; **~ seat** el asiento de niño

cash *v* cobrar; **~***n* el efectivo; **~ advance** sacar dinero de la tarjeta

change *v* **(buses)** transbordar; **~ *n* (money)** el cambio

cheap barato

Cheers! ¡Salud!

child el niño; **~ seat** la silla para niños

cigarette el cigarrillo

closed cerrado

conditioner el acondicionador

connect *v* **(internet)** conectarse

constipated estreñido

cook *v* cocinar

cool (temperature) frío
copper el cobre
corkscrew el sacacorchos
cute bonito

D

damage v causar daño
damaged ha sufrido daños
dance v bailar; ~ **club** la discoteca
dangerous peligroso
dark oscuro
date (calendar) la fecha
day el día
deaf sordo
debit card la tarjeta de débito
deck chair el camastro
declare v declarar
decline v **(credit card)** rechazar
deep hondo
degrees (temperature) los grados
delay v retrasar
delete v **(computer)** borrar
delicatessen la salchichonería
delicious delicioso
denim la mezclilla
dentist el dentista
denture la dentadura
deodorant el desodorante
department store las tiendas departamentales
departures (airport) las salidas

deposit *v* depositar; ~ *n* **(bank)** el depósito bancario; ~ *n* **(reserve a room)** el depósito

desert el desierto

dessert el postre

detergent el detergente

develop *v* **(film)** revelar

diabetic diabético

dial *v* marcar

diamond el diamante

diaper el pañal

diarrhea la diarrea

diesel el diésel

difficult difícil

digital digital; ~ **camera** la cámara digital; ~ **photos** las fotos digitales; ~ **prints** las fotos digitales

dining room el comedor

dinner la cena

direction la dirección

dirty sucio

disabled discapacitado

disconnect (computer) desconectar

discount el descuento

dish (kitchen) el plato; ~ **washer** el lavaplatos; ~ **washing liquid** el líquido lavaplatos

display *v* mostrar; ~ **case** la vitrina

disposable desechable; ~ **razor** la cuchilla desechable

dive *v* bucear

diving equipment el equipo de buceo

divorce *v* divorciar

dizzy mareado

doctor el doctor

doll la muñeca
dollar (U.S.) el dólar
domestic nacional; ~ **flight** el vuelo nacional
door la puerta
dormitory el dormitorio
double bed la cama matrimonial
downtown el centro
dozen la docena
dress (piece of clothing) el vestido; ~ **code** las normas de vestimenta
drink v beber; ~ n la bebida; ~ **menu** la carta de bebidas; ~**ing water** el agua potable
drive v conducir
driver's license number licencia de conducir
drop (medicine) la gota
drowsiness la somnolencia
dry cleaner la tintorería
dubbed doblado
during durante
duty (tax) el impuesto; ~**-free** libre de impuestos
DVD el DVD

E

ear la oreja; ~**ache** el dolor de oído
early temprano
earrings los aretes
east el este
easy fácil
eat v comer
economy class la clase turista
elbow el codo
electric outlet el enchufe

elevator el elevador

e-mail *v* enviar un correo electrónico; ~ *n* el correo electrónico; ~ **address** la dirección de correo electrónico

emergency la urgencia; ~ **exit** la salida de emergencia

empty *v* vaciar

end *v* terminar

English el inglés

engrave *v* grabar

enjoy *v* disfrutar

enter *v* entrar

entertainment el entretenimiento

entrance la entrada

envelope el sobre

equipment el equipo

e-ticket el boleto electrónico

evening la noche

exchange *v* (**money**) cambiar; ~ *v* (**goods**) devolver; ~ *n* (**place**) la casa de cambio; ~ **rate** el tipo de cambio

excursion la excursión

excuse *v* (**to get past**) pedir perdón; ~ *v* (**to get attention**) disculparse

exhausted agotado

exit *v* salir; ~ *n* la salida

expensive caro

expert (**skill level**) experto

express rápido;
 ~ **bus** el camión rápido; ~ **train** el tren rápido

extension (**phone**) la extensión

extra adicional; ~ **large** extra grande

extract *v* (**tooth**) extraer

eye el ojo

eyebrow wax la depilación de cejas

F

face la cara
facial el facial
family la familia
fan (appliance) el ventilador; ~ **(souvenir)** el abanico
far lejos; ~**-sighted** hipermétrope
farm la granja
fast rápido; ~ **food** la comida rápida
father el padre
fax v enviar un fax; ~ n el fax; ~ **number** el número de fax
fee la tarifa
feed v alimentar
ferry el transbordador
fever la fiebre
field (sports) la cancha
fill v llenar ; ~ **out** v (form) llenar
filling (tooth) la tapadura
fine (fee for breaking law) la multa
finger el dedo; ~ **nail** la uña
fire fuego; ~ **department** los bomberos; ~ **door** la puerta de incendios
first primero; ~ **class** la primera clase
fit (clothing) queda bien
fitting room el probador
fix v (repair) reparar
flashlight la linterna
flight el vuelo
floor el suelo
flower la flor
folk music la música folclórica
food la comida
foot el pie

football [BE] el fútbol

for para/por

forecast el pronóstico

forest el bosque

fork el tenedor

form el formulario

formula (baby) la fórmula

fort el fuerte

free gratuito

fresh fresco

friend el amigo

frying pan el sartén

full completo; **~-service** el servicio completo;
   ~-time de tiempo completo

G

game el partido

garage (parking) el garaje; **~ (repair)** el taller

garbage bag la bolsa de basura

gas la gasolina; **~ station** la gasolinera

gift el regalo; **~ shop** la tienda de regalos

girl la niña; **~ friend** la novia

glass (drinking) el vaso; **~ (material)** el vidrio

glasses los anteojos

go *v* **(somewhere)** ir a

good *n* el producto; **~** *adj* bueno

H

hat el sombrero

help *v* ayudar; **~***n* la ayuda

hospital el hospital

hot (temperature) caliente; **~ (spicy)** picante

hotel el hotel
hour la hora
house la casa; ~ **hold goods** los artículos para el hogar;
  ~ **keeping services** el servicio de limpieza de habitaciones
how (question) cómo; ~ **much (question)** cuánto cuesta
husband el esposo

I

identification la identificación
ill *v* **(to feel)** sentirse mal
in dentro
insurance el seguro
internet el Internet; ~ **cafe** el café Internet;
  ~ **service** el servicio de Internet;
  wireless ~ el acceso inalámbrico
Ireland Irlanda
Irish irlandés
iron *n* la plancha; ~ *v* **(clothes)** planchar

J

jacket la chamarra
jeans los jeans
jet ski la moto acuática
jewelry las joyas

K

key la llave; ~ **card** la llave electrónica; ~ **ring** el llavero
kiss *v* besar
knife el cuchillo

L

large grande

last último
late (time) tarde
laundry lavar ropa; ~ **service** el servicio de lavandería
lawyer el abogado
leather el cuero
left (direction) la izquierda
less menos
little chico
lose *v* **(something)** perder
love *v* querer; ~*n* el amor
lunch la comida

M

magazine la revista
magnificent magnífico
man el hombre
manager el gerente
Mexican mexicano
Mexico México
mistake el error
money el dinero
month el mes
more más
mother la madre

N

OK de acuerdo
north el norte
nothing nada
now ahora
number el número

O

OK de acuerdo
old viejo
once una vez
opposite frente a

P

pacifier el chupón
pack v hacer las maletas
please por favor
police la policía; ~ **report** la denuncia; ~ **station** la comisaría
pounds (British sterling) las libras esterlinas
pregnant embarazada
prescription la receta
press v (**clothing**) planchar
price el precio
print v imprimir
problem el problema
push v (**door sign**) empujar; ~**chair [BE]** el coche de niño

Q

quality la calidad
question la pregunta
quiet tranquilo

R

ready listo
real auténtico
receipt el recibo
receive v recibir
reception la recepción
recharge v recargar

recommend v recomendar
reserve v reservar
right (direction) derecha; ~ **of way** derecho de paso
room la habitación; ~ **key** la llave de habitación; ~ **service** el servicio al cuarto

S

sad triste
same mismo
school la escuela
scissors las tijeras
sea el mar
seat el asiento
see v ver
sick enfermo
sister la hermana
slow despacio
small chico
smoke v fumar
some alguno
soother [BE] el chupón
sore throat garganta irritada
sorry lo siento
south el sur
speak v hablar
stolen robado
study v estudiar
suitcase la maleta
sun el sol; ~ **block** el bloqueador solar; ~ **burn** la quemadura solar; ~ **glasses** los lentes oscuros; ~ **ny** soleado; ~ **screen** el protector solar

T

text *v* **(send a message)** enviar un mensaje de texto; ~ *n* **(message)** el texto
thank *v* dar las gracias a; ~ **you** gracias
that eso
thirsty sediento
this esto
tired cansado
tissue el pañuelo de papel
today hoy
toilet [BE] el sanitario; ~ **paper** el papel higiénico
tomorrow mañana
tonight esta noche
tooth el diente; ~ **brush** el cepillo de dientes; ~ **paste** la pasta de dientes
tough (food) duro
town la ciudad; ~ **hall** el ayuntamiento; ~ **map** el mapa de ciudad
travel *v* viajar; ~ **agency** la agencia de viajes; ~ **sickness** el mareo

U

ugly feo
umbrella el paraguas
underpants [BE] los calzones
understand *v* entender
United Kingdom (U.K.) el Reino Unido
United States (U.S.) los Estados Unidos

V

vacancy la habitación libre
vacation las vacaciones
valuable de valor

W

walk *v* caminar; ~*n* la caminata; **~ing route** la ruta de excursionismo
wallet la cartera
warm *v* calentar; ~ *adj* **(temperature)** calor
week la semana; **~end** el fin de semana; **~ly** semanal
well bien; **~-rested** descansado
west el oeste
who (question) quién
wife la esposa
wireless inalámbrico; ~ **internet** el acceso de Internet inalámbrico; ~
with con
without sin
woman la mujer
work *v* trabajar

Y

year el año
yes sí
yesterday ayer
young joven

Z

zoo el zoológico

Latin American Spanish

Essentials

Hello.	**¡Hola!** _oh_·lah
Goodbye.	**Adiós.** ah·_deeyohs_
Yes.	**Sí.** see
No.	**No.** noh
OK.	**De acuerdo.** deh ah·_kwehr_·doh
Excuse me! (to get attention)	**¡Disculpe!** dees·_kool_·peh
Excuse me. (to get past)	**Perdón.** pehr·_dohn_
I'm sorry.	**Lo siento.** loh _seeyehn_·toh
I'd like…	**Quiero…** _keeyeh_·roh…
How much?	**¿Cuánto?** _kwahn_·toh
Where is…?	**¿Dónde está…?** _dohn_·deh ehs·_tah_…
Please.	**Por favor.** pohr fah·_bohr_
Thank you.	**Gracias.** _grah_·seeyahs
You're welcome.	**De nada.** deh _nah_·dah
Please speak slowly.	**Hable más despacio, por favor.** _ah_·bleh mahs dehs·_pah_·seeyoh pohr fah·_bohr_
Can you repeat that?	**¿Podría repetir eso?** poh·_dree_·ah reh·peh·_teer_ eh·soh
I don't understand.	**No entiendo.** noh ehn·_teeyehn_·doh
Do you speak English?	**¿Habla usted inglés?** _ah_·blah oos·_ted_ een·_glehs_
I don't speak Spanish.	**No hablo español.** noh _ah_·bloh ehs·pah·_nyohl_
Where's the restroom [toilet]?	**¿Dónde están los servicios?** _dohn_·deh ehs·_tahn_ lohs sehr·_bee_·seeyohs
Help!	**¡Socorro!** soh·_koh_·rroh

You'll find the pronunciation of the Latin American Spanish letters and words written in gray after each sentence to guide you. Simply pronounce these as if they were English, noting that any underlines indicate an additional emphasis or stress or a lengthening of a vowel sound. As you hear the language being spoken, you will quickly become accustomed to the local pronunciation and dialect.

Numbers

0	**cero** _seh_•roh
1	**uno** _oo_•noh
2	**dos** dohs
3	**tres** trehs
4	**cuatro** _kwah_•troh
5	**cinco** _seen_•koh
6	**seis** seyees
7	**siete** _seeyeh_•teh
8	**ocho** _oh_•choh
9	**nueve** _nweh_•beh
10	**diez** deeyehs
11	**once** _ohn_•seh
12	**doce** _doh_•seh
13	**trece** _treh_•seh
14	**catorce** kah•_tohr_•seh
15	**quince** _keen_•seh
16	**dieciséis** deeyeh•see•_seyees_
17	**diecisiete** deeyeh•see•_seeyeh_•teh
18	**dieciocho** deeyeh•see•_oh_•choh
19	**diecinueve** deeyeh•see•_nweh_•beh

20	**veinte** _beyeen_·teh
21	**veintiuno** beyeen·tee·_oo_·noh
22	**veintidós** beyeen·tee·_dohs_
30	**treinta** _treyeen_·tah
31	**treinta y uno** _treyeen_·tah ee _oo_·noh
40	**cuarenta** kwah·_rehn_·tah
50	**cincuenta** seen·_kwehn_·tah
60	**sesenta** seh·_sehn_·tah
70	**setenta** seh·_tehn_·tah
80	**ochenta** oh·_chehn_·tah
90	**noventa** noh·_behn_·tah
100	**cien** seeyehn

Large numbers are read as in English. Example: 1,234,567
would be **un millón, doscientos treinta y cuatro mil,
quinientos sesenta y siete** (one million, two hundred thirty-four
thousand, five hundred sixty-seven). Notice the use of y (and) between
tens and units for numbers between 31 (**treinta y uno**; literally, thirty
and one) and 99 (**noventa y nueve**; literally, ninety and nine).

101	**ciento uno** <u>seeyehn</u>•toh <u>oo</u>•noh
200	**doscientos** dohs•<u>seeyehn</u>•tohs
500	**quinientos** kee•<u>neeyehn</u>•tohs
1,000	**mil** meel
10,000	**diez mil** deeyehs meel
1,000,000	**un millón** oon mee•<u>yohn</u>

Time

What time is it?	**¿Qué hora es?** keh <u>oh</u>•rah ehs
It's noon [midday].	**Son las doce del mediodía.** sohn lahs <u>doh</u>•seh dehl meh•deeyoh•<u>dee</u>•ah
At midnight.	**A medianoche.** ah meh•deeyah•<u>noh</u>•cheh
From one o'clock to two o'clock.	**De una a dos en punto.** deh <u>oo</u>•nah ah dohs ehn <u>poon</u>•toh

Latin Americans use the 24-hour clock when writing time, especially in schedules. The morning hours from 1:00 a.m. to noon are the same as in English. After that, just add 12 to the time: 1:00 p.m. would be 13:00, 5:00 p.m. would be 17:00 and so on.

Five after three.	**Las tres y cinco.** *lahs trehs ee seen·koh*
A quarter to five.	**Las cinco menos cuarto.** *lahs seen·koh meh·nohs kwahr·toh*
5:30 a.m./p.m.	**Las cinco y media de la mañana/tarde.** *lahs seen·koh ee meh·deeyah deh lah mah·nyah·nah/tahr·deh*

Days

Monday	**lunes** *loo·nehs*
Tuesday	**martes** *mahr·tehs*
Wednesday	**miércoles** *meeyehr·koh·lehs*
Thursday	**jueves** *khweh·behs*
Friday	**viernes** *beeyehr·nehs*
Saturday	**sábado** *sah·bah·doh*
Sunday	**domingo** *doh·meen·goh*

Dates

yesterday	**ayer** *ah·yehr*
today	**hoy** *oy*
tomorrow	**mañana** *mah·nyah·nah*
day	**día** *dee·ah*
week	**semana** *seh·mah·nah*
month	**mes** *mehs*
year	**año** *ah·nyoh*

Note that Spaniards often pronounce the **z** and the **c** before **i** or **e** like the "**th**" in "**thick**," while many Latin Americans pronounce it as the **s** in "**pleasure**".

Months

January	**enero** *eh·neh·roh*
February	**febrero** *feh·breh·roh*
March	**marzo** *mahr·soh*
April	**abril** *ah·breel*
May	**mayo** *mah·yoh*
June	**junio** *khoo·neeyoh*
July	**julio** *khoo·leeyoh*
August	**agosto** *ah·gohs·toh*
September	**septiembre** *sehp·teeyehm·breh*
October	**octubre** *ohk·too·breh*
November	**noviembre** *noh·beeyehm·breh*
December	**diciembre** *dee·seeyehm·breh*

Arrival & Departure

I'm here on vacation [holiday]/business.	**Estoy aquí de vacaciones/en viaje de negocios.** *ehs·toy ah·kee deh bah·kah·seeyohn·ehs/ehn beeyah·kheh deh neh·goh·seeyohs*
I'm going to…	**Voy a…** *boy ah…*
I'm staying at the… Hotel.	**Me alojo en el Hotel…** *meh ah·loh·khoh ehn ehl oh·tehl…*

Money

Where's…?	**¿Dónde está…?** *dohn·deh ehs·tah…*
the ATM	**el cajero automático** *ehl kah·kheh·roh awtoh·mah·tee·koh*
the bank	**el banco** *ehl bahn·koh*
the currency exchange office	**la casa de cambio** *lah kah·sah deh kahm·beeyoh*
When does the bank open/close?	**¿A qué hora abre/cierra el banco?** *ah keh oh·rah ah·breh/seeyeh·rrah ehl bahn·koh*

I'd like to change dollars/pounds into…

Quiero cambiar dólares/libras a…
keeyeh•roh kahm•_beeyahr doh_•lah•rehs/_lee_•brahs ah…

I'd like to cash traveler's checks [cheques].

Quiero cobrar cheques de viajero.
keeyeh•roh koh•_brahr cheh_•kehs deh beeyah•_kheh_•ro

YOU MAY SEE…

INTRODUCIR TARJETA AQUÍ	insert card here
CANCELAR	cancel
BORRAR	clear
INTRODUCIR	enter
CLAVE	PIN
RETIRAR FONDOS	withdraw funds
DE CUENTA CORRIENTE	from checking [current] account
DE CUENTA DE AHORROS	from savings account
RECIBO	receipt

Each country in Latin America has its own currency:

Argentina	peso argentino
Bolivia	peso boliviano
Chile	peso chileno
Colombia	peso colombiano
Costa Rica	colón costarricense
Cuba	peso cubano
Ecuador	dólar estadounidense (American dollar)
El Salvador	colón salvadoreño
Guatemala	quetzal
Honduras	lempira
Mexico	peso mexicano
Nicaragua	córdoba
Panama	balboa
Paraguay	guaraní
Peru	nuevo sol
Puerto Rico	dólar estadounidense (American dollar)
Dominican Republic	peso dominicano
Uruguay	peso uruguayo
Venezuela	bolívar

Getting Around

How do I get to town?	**¿Cómo se llega a la ciudad?** _koh·moh seh <u>yeh</u>·gah ah lah seew·<u>dahd</u>_
Where's...?	**¿Dónde está...?** _dohn·deh ehs·<u>tah</u>..._
the airport	**el aeropuerto** _ehl ah·eh·roh·<u>pwehr</u>·toh_
the train [railway] station	**la estación de tren** _lah ehs·tah·<u>seeyohn</u> deh trehn_
the bus station	**la estación de autobuses** _lah ehs·tah·<u>seeyohn</u> deh awtoh·<u>boo</u>·ses_
the metro [underground] station	**la estación de metro** _lah ehs·tah·<u>seeyohn</u> deh <u>meh</u>·troh_
How far is it?	**¿A qué distancia está?** _ah keh dees·<u>tahn</u>·seeyah ehs·<u>tah</u>_
Where do I buy a ticket?	**¿Dónde se compra el boleto?** _dohn·deh seh <u>kohm</u>·prah ehl boh·<u>leh</u>·toh_
A one-way/round-trip [return] ticket to...	**Un boleto de ida/ida y vuelta a...** _oon boh·<u>leh</u>·toh deh <u>ee</u>·dah/<u>ee</u>·dah ee <u>bwehl</u>·tah ah..._
How much?	**¿Cuánto es?** _kwahn·toh ehs_
Is there a discount?	**¿Hacen descuento?** _<u>ah</u>·sen dehs·<u>kwehn</u>·toh_

133

Which…?	**¿De qué…?** *deh keh…*
gate	**puerta de embarque** *pwehr·tah deh ehm·bahr·keh*
line	**línea** *lee·neh·ah*
platform	**andén** *ahn·dehn*
Where can I get a taxi?	**¿Dónde puedo tomar un taxi?** *dohn·deh pweh·doh toh·mahr oon tah·xee*
Take me to this address.	**Lléveme a esta dirección.** *yeh·beh·meh ah ehs·tah dee·rehk·seeyohn*
Where's the car rental [hire]?	**¿Dónde está el alquiler de autos?** *dohn·deh ehs·tah ehl ahl·kee·lehr deh ahoo·tohs*
Can I have a map?	**¿Podría darme un mapa?** *poh·dree·ah dahr·meh oon mah·pah*

The railway system is not fully developed in Latin America but most Latin American countries have a local and national rail service. Mexico and Argentina have almost no passenger rail service and are serviced by multiple private intercity bus lines. For more on bus transport, see page 28.

YOU MAY HEAR...

todo recto _toh·doh rehk·toh_	straight ahead
a la izquierda _ah lah ees·keeyehr·dah_	left
a la derecha _ah lah deh·reh·chah_	right
en/doblando la esquina _ehn/doh·blahn·doh lah ehs·kee·nah_	on/around the corner
frente a _frehn·teh ah_	opposite
detrás de _deh·trahs deh_	behind
al lado de _ahl lah·doh deh_	next to
después de _dehs·pwehs deh_	after
al norte/sur _ahl nohr·teh/soor_	north/south
al este/oeste _ahl ehs·teh/oh·ehs·teh_	east/west
en el semáforo _en ehl seh·mah·foh·roh_	at the traffic light
en el cruce _en ehl kroo·seh_	at the intersection

Tickets

When's…to Quito?	**¿Cuándo sale…a Quito?** _kwahn·doh sah·leh…ah kee·toh_
the (first) bus	**el (primer) autobús** _ehl (pree·mehr) awtoh·boos_
the (next) flight	**el (próximo) vuelo** _ehl (proh·xee·moh) bweh·loh_
the (last) train	**el (último) tren** _ehl (ool·tee·moh) trehn_
Where do I buy a ticket?	**¿Dónde se compra el boleto?** _dohn·deh seh kohm·prah ehl boh·leh·toh_
One/Two ticket(s), please.	**Un/Dos boleto(s), por favor.** _oon/dohs boh·leh·toh(s) pohr fah·bohr_
For today/tomorrow.	**Para hoy/mañana.** _pah·rah oy/mah·nyah·nah_
A…ticket.	**Un boleto…** _oon boh·leh·toh…_
one-way	**de ida** _deh ee·dah_
round-trip [return]	**de ida y vuelta** _deh ee·dah ee bwehl·tah_

Metro (subway) systems are not widespread in Latin America, and many cities do not have them. Buenos Aires (Argentina), Mexico City, Guadalajara and Monterrey (all in Mexico) are some cities that do have **metro** systems.

Metros in Latin America are easy to use and are reasonably priced. All **metro** systems operate on a one-way, per-ride basis.

first class	**de primera clase**	deh pree·*meh*·rah *klah*·she
business class	**clase ejecutiva**	*kla*·seh ehkhe·koo·*ti*·vah
economy class	**de clase económica**	deh *klah*·seh eh·koh·**noh**·mee·kah
How much?	**¿Cuánto es?**	*kwahn*·toh ehs
Is there a discount for…?	**¿Hacen descuento a…?**	*ah*·sehn dehs·*kwehn*·toh ah…
children	**los niños**	lohs *nee*·nyohs
students	**los estudiantes**	lohs ehs·too·*deeyahn*·tehs
senior citizens	**los jubilados**	lohs khoo·bee·*lah*·dohs
tourists	**turistas**	too·*rees*·tahs

YOU MAY SEE…

ANDENES	platforms
INFORMACIÓN	information
RESERVAS	reservations
SALA DE ESPERA	waiting room
LLEGADAS	arrivals
SALIDAS	departures

The express bus/express train, please.	**El autobús/tren exprés, por favor.**
	ehl ahoohtoh·boos/trehn ehx·prehs, pohr fah·bor
The local bus/train, please.	**El autobús/tren local, por favor.**
	ehl ahoohtoh·boos/trehn loh·kahl, pohr fah·bor
I have an e-ticket.	**Tengo un boleto electrónico.**
	tehn·goh oon boh·leh·toh eh·lehk·troh·nee·koh

The bus service in Latin American countries is extensive. For
local service within a town, you usually pay as you board the bus.
The fare will vary according to the length of the trip.

Note that buses can be called by various different names within a
country and these names can also vary from country to country:

Mexico	**camión, micro, pecera**
Peru	**micro, combi, bus**
Chile	**micro, liebre**
Central America	**camión, guagua**

Can I buy a ticket on the bus/train ?	**¿Puedo comprar el boleto a bordo del autobús/tren?** *pweh•doh kohm•prahr ehlbo•leh•toh ah bohr•doh dehl awtoh•boos/trehn*
Do I have to stamp the ticket before boarding?	**¿Tengo que sellar el boleto antes de abordar?** *tehn•goh keh sehyar ehl boh•leh•toh ahn•tes deh ah•bohr•dahr*
How long is this ticket valid?	**¿Cuál es la vigencia de este boleto?** *kwahl ehs lah vikhen•seeya deh ehs teh boh•leh•toh*
Can I return on the same ticket?	**¿Puedo volver con el mismo boleto?** *pweh•doh vohl•behr kohn ehl meez•moh boh•leh•toh*
I'd like to…my reservation.	**Quiero…mi reserva.** *keeyeh•roh…mee reh•sehr•bah*
cancel	**cancelar** *kahn•seh•lahr*

In Latin America there are some destinations with ferry service.
In Mexico, for example, there are ferries traveling from Cozumel
Island to Playa del Carmen, and from Isla Mujeres to Cancun. In
Argentina, there are ferries from Buenos Aires to Montevideo, Colonia
and Piriapolis (Uruguay).

| change | **cambiar** *kahm·<u>beeyahr</u>* |
| confirm | **confirmar** *kohn·feer·<u>mahr</u>* |

For Time, see page 128.

Car Hire

Where's the car rental [hire]?	**¿Dónde está el alquiler de autos?** *<u>dohn</u>·deh ehs·<u>tah</u> ehl ahl·kee·<u>lehr</u> deh <u>ahoo</u>·tohs*
I'd like...	**Quiero...** *<u>keeyeh</u>·roh...*
a cheap/small car	**un auto económico/pequeño** *oon <u>ahoo</u>·toh eh·koh·<u>noh</u>·mee·koh/peh·<u>keh</u>·nyoh*
an automatic/ a manual	**un auto automático/con transmisión manual** *oon <u>ahoo</u>·toh awtoh·<u>mah</u>·tee·koh/kohn trahnz·mee·<u>seeyohn</u> mah·noo·<u>ahl</u>*

In Spain and some Latin American countries, **coger** means to catch or get, e.g. **¿Dónde puedo coger un taxi?** (Where can I catch a cab?). However, in many countries in Latin America, **coger** is a vulgarity for 'to have sex'. Travelers to Latin America should always use **tomar**, e.g. **¿Dónde puedo tomar un taxi?**

air conditioning	**un auto con aire acondicionado** *oon* <u>*ahoo*</u>*·toh*	
	kohn <u>*ayee*</u>*·reh ah·kohn·dee·seeyoh·*<u>*nah*</u>*·doh*	
a car seat	**un asiento de niño** *oon ah·*<u>*seeyehn*</u>*·toh deh* <u>*nee*</u>*·nyoh*	
How much...?	**¿Cuánto cobran...?** <u>*kwahn*</u>*·toh* <u>*koh*</u>*·brahn...*	
per day/week	**por día/semana** *pohr* <u>*dee*</u>*·ah/seh·mah·nah*	
for...days	**por...días** *pohr...* <u>*dee*</u>*·ahs*	
per kilometer	**por kilómetro**	
	pohr kee·<u>*loh*</u>*·meh·troh*	

YOU MAY HEAR...

¿Tiene permiso de conducir internacional? Do you have an
<u>*teeyeh*</u>*·neh pehr·*<u>*mee*</u>*·soh deh kohn·doo·*<u>*seer*</u> international
een·tehr·nah·seeyoh·<u>*nahl*</u> driver's license?

Su pasaporte, por favor. Your passport,
soo pah·sah·<u>*pohr*</u>*·teh pohr fah·*<u>*bohr*</u> please.

¿Quiere seguro? <u>*keeyeh*</u>*·reh seh·*<u>*goo*</u>*·roh* Do you want insurance?

Tiene que dejar un depósito. <u>*teeyeh*</u>*·neh keh* I'll need a deposit.
deh·<u>*khahr*</u> *oon deh·*<u>*poh*</u>*·see·toh*

Firme aquí. <u>*feer*</u>*·meh ah·*<u>*kee*</u> Sign here.

for unlimited mileage	**por kilometraje ilimitado** *pohr kee·loh·meh·trah·kheh ee·lee·mee·tah·doh*
with insurance	**con el seguro** *kohn ehl seh·goo·roh*
Are there any discounts?	**¿Ofrecen algún descuento?** *oh·freh·sehn ahl·goon dehs·kwehn·toh*

Places to Stay

Can you recommend a hotel?	**¿Puede recomendarme un hotel?** *pweh·deh reh·koh·mehn·dahr·meh oon oh·tehl*
I have a reservation.	**Tengo una reserva.** *tehn·goh oo·nah reh·sehr·bah*
My name is…	**Me llamo…** *meh yah·moh…*
Do you have a room…?	**¿Tienen habitaciones…?** *teeyeh·nehn ah·bee·tah·seeyoh·nehs…*
for one/two	**individuales/dobles** *een·dee·bee·doo·ah·lehs/ doh·blehs*
with a bathroom	**con baño** *kohn bah·nyoh*
with air-conditioning	**con aire acondicionado** *kohn ayee· reh ah·kohn·dee·seeyoh·nah·doh*
For…	**Para…** *pah·rah…*
tonight	**esta noche** *ehs·tah noh·cheh*
two nights	**dos noches** *dohs noh·chehs*
one week	**una semana** *oo·nah seh·mah·nah*
How much?	**¿Cuánto es?** *kwahn·toh ehs*
Is there anything cheaper?	**¿Hay alguna tarifa más barata?** *aye ahl·goo·nah tah·ree·fah mahs bah·rah·tah*
When's check-out?	**¿A qué hora hay que desocupar la habitación?** *ah keh oh·rah aye keh deh·soh·koo·pahr lah ah·bee·tah·seeyohn*
Can I leave this in the safe?	**¿Puedo dejar esto en la caja fuerte?** *pweh·doh deh·khahr ehs·toh ehn lah kah·khah fwehr·teh*

When asking for a public restroom, it's more common and polite to use the term **servicio**. The term **baño** tends to be used when asking for a private bathroom such as in a home or a hotel room. Native speakers sometimes use both words interchangeably, but you will almost always see **servicio** on a sign.

Can I leave my bags?	**¿Podría dejar mi equipaje?** *poh·dree·ah deh· khahr mee eh·kee·pah·kheh*
Can I have the bill/ a receipt?	**¿Me da la factura/un recibo?** *meh dah lah fahk·too·rah/oon reh·see·boh*
I'll pay in cash/by credit card.	**Voy a pagar en efectivo/con tarjeta de crédito.** *boy ah pah·gahr ehn eh·fehk·tee·boh/kohn tahr·kheh·tah deh kreh·dee·toh*

YOU MAY SEE...

EMPUJAR/TIRAR	push/pull
BAÑO/SERVICIO	bathroom/restroom [toilet]
DUCHA	shower
ASCENSOR	elevator [lift]
ESCALERAS	stairs
LAVANDERÍA	laundry
NO MOLESTAR	do not disturb
PUERTA DE INCENDIOS	fire door
SALIDA (DE EMERGENCIA)	exit (emergency)

Communications

Where's an internet cafe?	**¿Dónde hay un cibercafé?** _dohn_•deh aye oon see•behr•kah•_feh_
Can I access the internet here/ check e-mail ?	**¿Puedo acceder a Internet/revisar el correo electrónico?** _pweh_•doh ahk•seh•_dehr_ ah een•tehr•_neht_/reh•bee•_sahr_ ehl koh•_rreh_•oh eh•lehk•_troh_•nee•koh
How much per (half) hour?	**¿Cuánto cuesta por (media) hora?** _kwahn_•toh _kwehs_•tah pohr (_meh_•deeyah) _oh_•rah
How do I connect/ log on?	**¿Cómo entro al sistema/inicio la sesión?** _koh_•moh _ehn_•troh ahl sees•_teh_•mah/ee•_nee_•seeyoh lah seh•_seeyohn_
A phone card, please.	**Una tarjeta telefónica, por favor.** _oo_•nah tahr•_kheh_•tah teh•leh•_foh_•nee•kah pohr fah•_bohr_
Can I have your phone number?	**¿Me puede dar su número de teléfono?** meh _pweh_•deh dahr soo _noo_•meh•roh deh teh•_leh_•foh•noh
Here's my number/ e-mail address.	**Aquí tiene mi número/dirección de correo electrónico.** ah•_kee_ _teeyeh_•neh mee _noo_•meh•roh/ dee•rehk•_seeyohn_ deh koh•_rreh_•oh eh•lehk•_troh_•nee•koh
Call me.	**Llámeme.** _yah_•meh•meh

143

E-mail me.	**Envíeme un correo.** *ehn·bee·eh·meh oon koh·rreh·oh*
Hello. This is…	**Hola. Soy…** *oh·lah soy…*
Can I speak to…?	**¿Puedo hablar con…?** *pweh·doh ah·blahr kohn…*
Can you repeat that?	**¿Puede repetir eso?** *pweh·deh reh·peh·teer eh·soh*
I'll call back later.	**Llamaré más tarde.** *yah·mah·reh mahs tahr·deh*
Bye.	**Adiós.** *ah·deeyohs*
Where's the post office?	**¿Dónde está la oficina de correos?** *dohn·deh ehs·tah lah oh·fee·see·nah deh koh·rreh·ohs*

Public phones are generally either coin or card operated, though coin operated phones are becoming less common. Phone cards can be purchased in post offices, newsstands and supermarkets. For international calls, calling cards are the most economical. You can also make long distance calls at **locutorios** (call centers); these also offer internet, fax and wireless phone charging services at reasonable prices. International hotel call rates can be very expensive. To call the U.S. or Canada from Latin America, dial 00 + 1 + area code + phone number. To call the U.K. from Latin America, dial 00 + 44 + area code (minus the first 0) + phone number.

Oficinas de Correos (post offices) in Latin America offer more than just standard postal services. You may be able to fax, scan and e-mail documents and send money orders from the local post office. The services available vary by location.

I'd like to send this to...	**Quiero mandar esto a...** _keeyeh_•roh _mahn_•dahr ehs•toh ah...

Social Media

Are you on Facebook /Twitter?	**¿Estás en Facebook/Twitter?** ehs•_tahs_ ehn _fays_•book/_twee_•tehr
What's your user name?	**¿Cuál es tu nombre de usuario?** kwahl ehs too _nohm_•breh deh oo•_swah_•reeoh
I'll add you as a friend.	**Te agregaré como amigo(a).** teh ah•greh•gah•_reh_ koh•moh ah•_mee_•goh(ah)
I'll follow you on Twitter.	**Te seguiré en Twitter.** teh seh•gee•_reh_ ehn twee•tehr
Are you following...?	**¿Estás siguiendo...?** ehs•_tahs_ see•_geeyehn_•doh
I'll put the pictures on Facebook/Twitter.	**Pondré fotos en Facebook/Twitter.** pohn•_dreh_ _foh_•tohs ehn _fays_•book/_twee_•tehr
I'll tag you in the pictures.	**Te etiquetaré en las fotos.** teh eh•tee•keh•tah•_reh_ ehn lahs _foh_•tohs

Conversation

Hello!	**¡Hola!** _oh_•lah
How are you?	**¿Cómo está?** _koh_•moh ehs•_tah_
Fine, thanks.	**Bien, gracias.** beeyehn _grah_•seeyahs
Excuse me! (to get attention)	**¡Disculpe!** dihs•_koohl_•peh
Do you speak English?	**¿Habla inglés?** _ah_•blah een•_glehs_

145

YOU MAY SEE...

CERRAR	close
BORRAR	delete
CORREO ELECTRÓNICO	e-mail
SALIR	exit
AYUDA	help
MENSAJERO INSTANTÁNEO	instant messenger
INTERNET	internet
INICIO DE SESIÓN	login
NUEVO (MENSAJE)	new (message)
ENCENDER/APAGAR	on/off
ABRIR	open
IMPRIMIR	print
GUARDAR	save
ENVIAR	send
NOMBRE DE USUARIO/CONTRASEÑA	username/password
INTERNET INALÁMBRICO	wireless internet

What's your name?	**¿Cómo se llama?** _koh·moh seh yah·mah_
My name is...	**Me llamo...** _meh yah·moh..._
Nice to meet you.	**Encantado _m_/Encantada _f._** _ehn·kahn·tah·doh/ ehn·kahn·tah·dah_
Where are you from?	**¿De dónde es usted?** _deh dohn·deh ehs oos·tehd_
I'm from the U.S./U.K.	**Soy de Estados Unidos/del Reino Unido.** _soy deh ehs·tah·dohs oo·nee·dohs/dehl reyee·noh oo·nee·doh_
What do you do?	**¿A qué se dedica?** _ah keh seh deh·dee·kah_
I work for...	**Trabajo para...** _trah·bah·khoh pah·rah..._
I'm a student.	**Soy estudiante.** _soy ehs·too·deeyahn·teh_

YOU MAY HEAR...

Hablo muy poco inglés.
_ah_•bloh mooy _poh_•koh een•_glehs_

I only speak a little English.

No hablo inglés. noh _ah_•bloh een•_glehs_

I don't speak English.

I'm retired.	**Estoy jubilado** _m_**/jubilada** _f._
	ehs•_toy_ khoo•bee•_lah_•doh/khoo•bee•_lah_•dah
Do you like...?	**¿Le gusta...?** leh _goos_•tah...
Goodbye.	**Adiós.** ah•_deeyohs_
See you later.	**Hasta luego.** _ah_•stah _lweh_•goh

Romance

Would you like to go out for a drink/dinner?	**¿Le gustaría salir a tomar una copa/cenar?**
	leh goos•tah•_ree_•ah sah•_leer_ ah toh•_mahr_
	_oo_•nah _koh_•pah/seh•_nahr_
What are your plans for tonight/tomorrow?	**¿Qué planes tiene para esta noche/mañana?**
	keh _plah_•nehs _teeyeh_•neh _pah_•rah ehs•tah _noh_•cheh/
	mah•_nyah_•nah

When first meeting someone in Latin America always greet him or her with **hola** (hello), **buenos días** (good morning) or **buenas tardes** (good afternoon). Latin Americans even extend this general greeting to strangers when in elevators, waiting rooms and other small public spaces. A general acknowledgment or reply is expected from all. When leaving, say **adiós** (goodbye).

Can I have your number?	**¿Puede darme su número?** _pweh_·deh _dahr_·meh soo _noo_·meh·roh
Can I join you?	**¿Puedo acompañarlo m/acompañarla f?** _pweh_·doh ah·kohm·pah·_nyahr_·loh/ah·kohm·pah·_nyahr_·lah
Can I buy you a drink?	**¿Puedo invitarle una copa?** _pweh_·doh een·bee·_tahr_·leh _oo_·nah _koh_·pah
I like you.	**Me gustas.** meh _goos_·tahs
I love you.	**Te quiero.** teh _keeyeh_·roh

Accepting & Rejecting

I'd love to.	**Me encantaría.** *meh ehn•kahn•tah•<u>ree</u>•yah*
Where should we meet?	**¿Dónde nos encontramos?** *<u>dohn</u>•deh nohs en•kohn•<u>trah</u>•mohs*
I'll meet you at the bar/your hotel.	**Nos encontramos en el bar/su hotel.** *nohs en•kohn•<u>trah</u>•mohs ehn ehl bahr/soo oh•<u>tehl</u>*
I'll come by at…	**Pasaré a recogerlo m/recogerla f a las…** *pah•sah•<u>reh</u> ah reh•koh•<u>khehr</u>•loh/ reh•koh•<u>khehr</u>•lah ah lahs…*
What is your address?	**¿Cuál es su dirección?** *kwahl ehs soo dee•rehk•<u>seeyohn</u>*
I'm busy.	**Estoy ocupado m/ocupada f.** *ehs•<u>toy</u> oh•koo•<u>pah</u>•doh/oh•koo•<u>pah</u>•dah*
I'm not interested.	**No me interesa.** *noh meh een•teh•<u>reh</u>•sah*
Leave me alone.	**Déjeme en paz.** *<u>deh</u>•kheh•meh ehn pahs*
Stop bothering me!	**¡Deje de molestarme!** *deh•kheh <u>deh</u> moh•lehs•<u>tahr</u>•meh*

149

Food & Drink

Eating Out

Can you recommend a good restaurant/bar?	**¿Puede recomendarme un buen restaurante/bar?** *pweh·deh reh·koh·mehn·dahr·meh oon bwehn rehs·taw·rahn·teh/bahr*
Is there a traditional/inexpensive restaurant nearby?	**¿Hay un restaurante típico/barato cerca de aquí?** *aye oon rehs·taw·rahn·teh tee·pee·koh/bah·rah·toh sehr·kah deh ah·kee*
A table for one/two, please.	**Una mesa para uno/dos…, por favor.** *oo·nah meh·sah pah·rah oo·noh/dohs pohr fah·bohr*
Can we sit…?	**¿Podemos sentarnos…?** *poh·deh·mohs sehn·tahr·nohs…*
here/there	**aquí/allá** *ah·kee/ah·ya*
outside	**afuera** *ah·fweh·rah*
in a non-smoking area	**en una zona de no fumadores** *ehn oo·nah soh·nah deh noh foo·mah·doh·rehs*
I'm waiting for someone.	**Estoy esperando a alguien.** *ehs·toy ehs·peh·rahn·doh ah ahl·geeyehn*
Where's the restroom [toilet]?	**¿Dónde están los servicios?** *dohn·deh ehs·tahn lohs sehr·bee·seeohs*
A menu, please.	**Una carta, por favor.** *oo·nah kahr·tah pohr fah·bohr*
What do you recommend?	**¿Qué me recomienda?** *keh meh reh·koh·meeyehn·dah*

YOU MAY SEE…

PROPINA	cover charge
MENÚ DEL DÍA	menu of the day
SERVICIO (NO) INCLUIDO	service (not) included
ESPECIALIDADES DE LA CASA	specials

Although restaurants are generally required to include service charges as part of the bill, a tip is also expected. A tip of 10% of the bill is customary for the waiter.

I'd like…	**Quiero…** _keeyeh_·roh…
Some more…, please.	**Quiero más…, por favor.** _keeyeh_·roh mahs…pohr fah·_bohr_
Enjoy your meal!	**¡Buen provecho!** bwen proh·_beh_·choh
The check [bill], please.	**La cuenta, por favor.** lah _kwen_·tah pohr fah·_bohr_
Is service included?	**¿Está incluido el servicio?** ehs·_tah_ een·kloo·_ee_·doh ehl sehr·_bee_·seeyoh
Can I pay by credit card?	**¿Puedo pagar con tarjeta de crédito?** _pweh_·doh pah·_gahr_ kohn tahr·_kheh_·tah deh _kreh_·dee·toh
Can I have a receipt?	**¿Podría darme un recibo?** poh·dree·ah _dahr_·meh oon reh·_see_·boh
Thank you!	**¡Gracias!** _grah_·seeyahs

Breakfast

el tocino *ehl toh•see•noh*		bacon
el pan *ehl pahn*		bread
la mantequilla *lah mahn•teh•kee•yah*		butter
el queso *ehl keh•soh*		cheese
el huevo… *ehl weh•boh…*		egg…
duro/pasado por agua *doo•roh/ pah•sah•doh pohr ah•gwah*		hard-/soft-boiled
frito *free•toh*		fried
revuelto *reh•bwehl•toh*		scrambled
la mermelada/la jalea *lah mehr•meh•lah•dah/khah•leh•ah*		jam/jelly
la tortilla… *lah tohr•tee•yah…*		omelet
la tostada *lah tohs•tah•dah*		toast

El desayuno (breakfast) is usually served from 7:00 – 10:00 a.m. **El almuerzo** (lunch), generally the largest meal of the day, is served from 1:00– 4:00 p.m. **La cena** (dinner) is typically a light meal, and is usually served after 8:00 p.m.

el yogur *ehl yoh·goor*   yogurt
la salchicha *lah sahl·chee·chah*   sausage

Appetizers

las aceitunas (rellenas)   (stuffed) olives
lahs ah·seyee·too·nahs (reh·yeh·nahs)
las albóndigas *lahs ahl·bohn·dee·gahs*   meatballs
las anchoas en vinagre   anchovies marinated
lahs an·choh·ahs ehn bee·nah·greh   in garlic and olive oil
el bacalao *ehl bah·kah·laoh*   dried salt cod
las brochetas *lahs broh·cheh·tahs*   grilled, skewered meat
los caracoles *lohs kah·rah·koh·lehs*   snails
el ceviche *ehl seh·bee·cheh*   raw fish marinated in lime
los champiñones al ajillo   mushrooms fried in
lohs chahm·pee·nyoh·nehs ahl ah·khee·yoh   olive oil with garlic
las croquetas *lahs kroh·keh·tahs*   croquettes with various
                                                fillings
las empanadas... *lahs ehm·pah·nah·dahs...* flour dough stuffed...
  de carne *deh kahr·neh*   with meat
  de pollo *deh poh·yoh*   with chicken
  de queso *deh keh·soh*   with cheese
las langostinos al ajillo   broiled shrimp in
lohs lahn·gohs·tee·nohs ahl ah·khee·yoh   garlic
el mondongo *ehl mon·dohn·goh*   tripe in hot paprika sauce
los pescados fritos *lohs pehs·kah·dohs free·tohs* fried fish
los pimientos *lohs pee·meeyehn·tohs*   peppers
los quesos *lohs keh·sohs*   cheese platter
el tamal *ehl tah·mahl*   corn and cornmeal dough
                                                stuffed with a meat mixture
la tortilla española   potato omelet
lah tohr·tee·yah ehs·pah·nyoh·lah

YOU MAY HEAR...

muy poco cocido *m*/cocida *f*   rare
mooy poh·koh koh·sih·doh/koh·sih·dah

término medio *tehr·meeh·noh meh·deeyoh*   medium

bien cocido *m*/cocida *f*
beeyehn koh·sih·doh/koh·sih·dah   well-done

Meat

la carne de res *lah kahr·neh deh rehs*	beef
la carne molida *lah kahr·neh moh·lee·dah*	ground beef
el pollo *ehl poh·yoh*	chicken
el cordero *ehl kohr·deh·roh*	lamb
la carne de cerdo *lah kahr·neh deh sehr·doh*	pork
el bisté *ehl bees·teh*	beef steak
la ternera *lah tehr·neh·rah*	veal

Argentina is famous for its **asado**, or barbecued meat.
The **asado** is a typical food all over the country. It includes
several different cuts of beef and sometimes includes chicken, and
occasionally pork.
Asado is typically spiced with **chimichurri**, a sauce made with garlic,
red pepper, parsley, hot pepper, onion, thyme, and bay leaves. It is
usually served with red wine.

Fish & Seafood

el bacalao *ehl bah·kah·laoh*	cod
el cangrejo *ehl kahn·greh·khoh*	crab
el arenque *ehl ah·rehn·keh*	herring
la langosta *lah lahn·gohs·tah*	lobster
los mejillones *lohs meh·khee·yoh·nehs*	mussels
el pulpo *ehl pool·poh*	octopus
la ostra *lah ohs·trah*	oyster
el salmón *ehl sahl·mohn*	salmon

Ceviche is a specialty dish of many Latin American countries. It is made by marinating raw fish with lemons and limes. The citrus adds flavor and cooks the fish without heat. The preparation includes onions and hot peppers, and it can be served with corn and sweet potato. **Ceviche** is always served cold.

There are many different kinds of **ceviche** depending on the country or city. The most well-known is the one made with fish. However you can also find **ceviche** made with shellfish, squid and shrimp.

el lenguado *ehl lehn·<u>gwah</u>·doh*	sole
el tiburón *ehl tee·boo·<u>rohn</u>*	shark
los langostinos *lohs lahn·<u>gohs</u>·tee·nohs*	shrimp
el pez espada *ehl pehs ehs·<u>pah</u>·dah*	swordfish
la trucha *lah <u>troo</u>·chah*	trout

Vegetables

los frijoles *lah free·<u>kho</u>·lehs*	beans
las habas *lahs <u>ah</u>·bahs*	broad beans
la vainita *lah bahy·<u>nee</u>·tah*	green bean
el repollo *ehl reh·<u>poh</u>·yoh*	cabbage
la zanahoria *lah sah·nah·<u>oh</u>·reeyah*	carrot
el hongo *ehl <u>ohn</u>·goh*	mushroom
la cebolla *lah seh·<u>boh</u>·yah*	onions
la arveja *lah ar·<u>beh</u>·kha*	pea
la pimienta negra *lah pee·<u>meeyehn</u>·tah<u>neh</u>·grah*	black pepper
el pimiento relleno *ehl pee·<u>meeyehn</u>·toh reh·<u>yeh</u>·noh*	stuffed pepper
el pimiento rojo/verde *ehl pee·<u>meeyehn</u>·toh <u>roh</u>·khoh/<u>behr</u>·deh*	red/green pepper

la papa *lah <u>pah</u>·pah*	potato
el tomate *ehl toh·**mah**·teh*	tomatoes

Sauces & Condiments

la sal *lah sahl*	salt
pimienta *pee·**meeyehn**·tah*	pepper
mostaza *mohs·<u>tah</u>·sah*	mustard
cátsup *<u>kaht</u>·soop*	ketchup

Fruit & Dessert

la manzana *lah mahn·<u>sah</u>·nah*	apple
la banana *lah bah·<u>nah</u>·nah*	banana
el limón *ehl lee·mohn*	lemon
la naranja *lah nah·<u>rahn</u>·khah*	orange
la pera *lah <u>peh</u>·rah*	pear
la fresa *lah <u>freh</u>·sah*	strawberriy
el alfajor *ehl ahl·fah·<u>khor</u>*	sweet dough filled with caramel and sprinkled with powder sugar
el arroz con leche *ehl ah·<u>rros</u> kohn <u>leh</u>·cheh*	rice pudding
el brazo de gitano *ehl <u>brah</u>·soh deh khee· <u>tah</u>·noh*	sponge cake roll with cream filling
el buñuelo *ehl boo·<u>nyweh</u>·loh*	thin, deep-fried fritter, covered in sugar
el churro *ehl <u>choo</u>·rroh*	deep-fried fritter sprinkled with sugar
el dulce de leche *ehl <u>dool</u>·seh deh <u>leh</u>·cheh*	cooked sugared milk
el flan *ehl flahn*	caramel custard
la galleta *lah gah·<u>yeh</u>·tah*	cookie [biscuit]
la gelatina *lah geh·lah·<u>tee</u>·nah*	jello® [jelly]
el helado *ehl eh·<u>lah</u>·doh*	ice cream
la leche frita *lah <u>leh</u>·cheh <u>free</u>·tah*	fried milk custard

la mantecada *lah mahn•teh•kah•dah* — small sponge cake

la manzana asada *lah mahn•sah•nah ah•sah•dah* — baked apple

el panqueque *ehl pahn•keh•keh* — crepe (used in sweet or savory dishes)

el pastel de manzana *ehl pahs•tehl deh mahn•sah•nah* — apple pie

el pastel de queso *ehl pahs•tehl deh keh•soh* — cheesecake

el pie de limón *ehl pah•ee deh lee•mohn* — keylime pie

el sorbete *ehl sohr•beh•teh* — sorbet

Drinks

The wine list/drink menu, please.	**La carta de vinos/bebidas, por favor.** *kahr•tah deh bee•nohs/beh•bee•dahs pohr fah•bohr*
What do you recommend?	**¿Qué me recomienda?** *keh meh reh•koh•meeyehn•dah*
I'd like a bottle/glass of red/white wine.	**Quiero una botella/una copa de vino tinto/blanco.** *keeyeh•roh oo•nah boh•teh•yah/oo•nah koh•pah deh bee•noh teen•toh/blahn•koh*
The house wine, please.	**El vino de la casa, por favor.** *ehl bee•noh deh lah kah•sah pohr fah•bohr*

Another bottle/glass, please.	**Otra botella/Otra copa, por favor.**	_oh·trah boh·teh·yah/oh·trah koh·pah pohr fah·bohr_
I'd like a local beer.	**Quiero una cerveza local.**	_keeyeh·roh oo·nah sehr·beh·sah loh·khal_
Let me buy you a drink.	**¿Puedo invitarle a una copa?**	_pweh·doh een·bee·tahr·leh ah oo·nah koh·pah_
Cheers!	**¡Salud!**	_sah·lood_
A coffee/tea, please.	**Un café/té, por favor.**	_oon kah·feh/teh pohr fah·bohr_
Black coffee.	**Café solo.**	_kah·feh soh·loh_
With…	**Con…**	_kohn…_
milk	**leche**	_leh·cheh_

There are many popular brands of beer in Latin America, such as **Águila®** in Colombia, **Polar®** in Venezuela and **Quilmes®** in Argentina. Each brand usually has several classes and types of beer available, though most will be a lager-type beer.

The classes of beer include **clásica**, a light, pale, pilsner-type lager; **especial**, a heavier pilsner-type lager; **negra**, a dark, malty lager; and **extra**, a heavy, high-alcohol lager.

Many Latin Americans love coffee and drink it throughout the day.
Tap water is not always safe to drink, though many locals drink it
at home. Travelers are recommended always to drink bottled water.
Restaurants will almost always serve bottled water with meals, unless
you specifically request **agua del grifo**, tap water.
Juice is usually served with breakfast, but it's not common to drink it at
lunch or dinner.

sugar	**azúcar** ah·_soo_·kahr	
artificial sweetener	**edulcorante artificial**	
	eh·dool·khoh·_rahn_·teh ahr·tee·fee·_seeyahl_	
A..., please.	**Un..., por favor.** oon...pohr fah·_bohr_	
juice	**jugo** _khoo_·goh	
soda	**refresco** reh·_frehs_·koh	
(sparkling/still)	**agua (con/sin gas)** _ah_·gwah (kohn/seen gahs)	
water		

Latin America has many land areas under vine. Chile is probably
the most famous wine-producing country in Latin America. Their
wine culture has existed for centuries and there is a wide selection of
global wine varieties.
In Latin America, vineyards are called **viñedos** and the chambers
where the wine is kept are called **bodegas**.

Leisure Time

Sightseeing

Where's the tourist information office?	**¿Dónde está la oficina de turismo?** _dohn_•deh ehs•_tah_ lah oh•fee•_see_•nah deh too•_reez_•moh
What are the main attractions?	**¿Dónde están los principales sitios de interés?** _dohn_•deh ehs•_tahn_ lohs preen•see•_pah_•lehs _see_•teeyohs deh een•teh•_rehs_
Do you have tours in English?	**¿Hay visitas en inglés?** aye bee•_see_•tahs ehn een•_glehs_
Can I have a map/guide?	**¿Puede darme un mapa/una guía?** _pweh_•deh _dahr_•meh oon _mah_•pah/_oo_•nah _gee_•ah

Tourist offices are located in major Latin American cities and in many of the smaller towns that are popular tourist attractions. Ask at your hotel or check online to find the nearest office.

Shopping

Where's the market/mall [shopping centre]?	**¿Dónde está el mercado/centro comercial?** _dohn•deh ehs•tah ehl mehr•kah•doh/sen•troh koh•mehr•seeyahl_
I'm just looking.	**Sólo estoy mirando.** _soh•loh ehs•toy mee•rahn•doh_
Can you help me?	**¿Puede ayudarme?** _pweh•deh ah•yoo•dahr•meh_
I'm being helped.	**Ya me atienden.** _yah meh ah•teeyehn•dehn_
How much?	**¿Cuánto es?** _kwahn•toh ehs_
That one, please.	**Ése _m_/Ésa _f_, por favor.** _eh•she/eh•sah pohr fah•bohr_
That's all.	**Eso es todo.** _eh•soh ehs toh•doh_

YOU MAY SEE...

HORARIO DE APERTURA	Opening hours
CERRADO POR HORARIO DE COMIDA	Closed for lunch
PROBADORES	Fitting room
CAJERO/CAJERA	Cashier
SOLO EFECTIVO	Cash only
SE ACEPTAN TARJETAS DE CRÉDITO	Credit cards accepted

Credit cards are widely accepted throughout Latin America; you will need to show ID when using a credit card. Mastercard™ and Visa™ are the most commonly used; American Express® is accepted in most places. Debit cards are also commonly used; these are usually accepted if backed by Visa™ or Mastercard™. Traveler's checks cannot be used everywhere. Cash is always accepted — some places, such as newsstands, tobacconists, flower shops and market or street stands, take cash only.

Where can I pay?	**¿Dónde se paga?** <u>dohn</u>·deh seh <u>pah</u>·gah
I'll pay in cash/by credit card.	**Voy a pagar en efectivo/con tarjeta de crédito.** boy ah pah·<u>gahr</u> ehn eh·<u>fehk</u>·tee·boh/kohn tahr·<u>kheh</u>·tah deh <u>kreh</u>·dee·toh
A receipt, please.	**Un recibo, por favor.** oon reh·<u>see</u>·boh pohr fah·<u>bohr</u>

Sport & Leisure

When's the game?	**¿Cuándo empieza el partido?** <u>kwahn</u>·doh ehm·<u>peeyeh</u>·sah ehl pahr·<u>tee</u>·doh
Where's...?	**¿Dónde está...?** <u>dohn</u>·deh ehs·<u>tah</u>...
the beach	**la playa** lah <u>plah</u>·yah
the park	**el parque** ehl <u>pahr</u>·keh

Fútbol (soccer) is the most popular sport in Latin America; most of the countries in Latin America have their own professional teams with a large fan base. Note that fans are extremely dedicated, so be sure not to insult the team.
Other popular sports include basketball, tennis, auto racing and golf.

Leisure Time

the pool	**la piscina** *lah pees·see·nah*
Is it safe to swim here?	**¿Es seguro nadar aquí?** *ehs seh·goo·roh nah·dahr ah·kee*
Can I rent [hire] golf clubs?	**¿Puedo alquilar palos de golf?** *pweh·doh ahl·kee·lahr pah·lohs deh golf*
How much per hour?	**¿Cuánto cuesta por hora?** *kwahn·toh kwehs·tah pohr oh·rah*
How far is it to…?	**¿A qué distancia está…?** *ah keh dees·tahn·seeyah ehs·tah…*
Can you show me on the map, please?	**¿Puede indicármelo en el mapa, por favor?** *pweh·deh een·dee·kahr·meh·loh ehn ehl mah·pah pohr fah·bohr*

There is no shortage of great skiing in Latin America. The Andes in South America is the longest mountain range in the world, forming a continuous chain along the west. It is over 4,400 miles (7,000 km) long. The mountains extend over seven countries: Argentina, Bolivia, Chile, Colombia, Ecuador, Peru and Venezuela. The highest peak in the Andes is the Aconcagua in Argentina which reaches 22,841 feet (6,962 m).

Coastal countries in Latin America have many miles of coastline
and beaches. The Dominican Republic, on the Caribbean Sea,
boasts some of the most beautiful beaches in the world. Cuba,
Venezuela, Mexico and Colombia also have world-famous beaches. If
you decide to go for a swim, check the safety flags at each beach. Green
flags indicate the water is safe, yellow flags indicate that you should use
caution and red flags indicate that the water is unsafe for swimming.

Going Out

What's there to do at night?	**¿Qué se puede hacer por las noches?** _keh seh pweh·deh ah·sehr pohr lahs noh·chehs_
Do you have a program of events?	**¿Tiene un programa de espectáculos?** _teeyeh·neh oon proh·grah·mah deh ehs·pehk·tah·koo·lohs_
What's playing tonight?	**¿Qué hay en cartelera esta noche?** _keh aye ehn kahr·teh·leh·rah ehs·tah noh·cheh_
Where's…?	**¿Dónde está…?** _dohn·deh ehs·tah…_
the arcade?	**la galería?** _lah gah·leh·ree·ah_
the downtown area	**el centro** _ehl sehn·troh_

One of Argentina's greatest cultural achievements is the tango. Tango is a social dance that originated in Buenos Aires in Argentina. The musical styles that evolved together with the dance are also known as 'tango'.

Music and dance elements of tango are also popular in activities related to dancing such as figure skating and synchronized swimming because of its dramatic expression and its cultural associations with romance and love.

In Argentina, you may want to visit one of the many tango clubs, and you can even learn how to dance.

the bar	**el bar**	*ehl bahr*
the dance club	**la discoteca**	*lah dees·koh·teh·kah*
Is there a cover charge?	**¿Hay que pagar entrada?** *aye keh pah·gahr ehn·trah·dah*	

There are many casinos throughout Latin America. Minimum entrance and gaming age is 18; ID is required and the dress code is business casual.

Baby Essentials

Do you have…?	**¿Tiene…?** _teeyeh_•neh…
a baby bottle	**un biberón** _oon bee•beh•rohn_
baby wipes	**toallitas** _toh•ah•yee•tahs_
a car seat	**un asiento para niños** _oon ah•seeyehn•toh pah•rah nee•nyohs_
a children's menu/portion	**un menú/una ración para niños** _oon meh•noo/ oo•nah rah•seeyohn pah•rah nee•nyohs_
a child's seat/ highchair	**una silla para niños/alta** _oo•nah see•yah pah•rah nee•nyohs/ahl•tah_
a crib/cot	**una cuna/un catre** _oo•nah koo•nah/oon kah•treh_
diapers [nappies]	**pañales** _pah•nyah•lehs_
formula	**fórmula infantil** _fohr•moo•lah een•fahn•teel_
a pacifier [soother]	**un chupete** _oon choo•peh•teh_
a playpen	**un parque** _oon pahr•keh_
a stroller [pushchair]	**un coche** _oon koh•cheh_
Can I breastfeed the baby here?	**¿Puedo darle de lactar al bebé aquí?** _pweh•doh dahr•leh deh lahk•tahr ahl beh•beh ah•kee_
Where can I change the baby?	**¿Dónde puedo cambiar al bebé?** _dohn•deh pweh•doh kahm•beeyahr ahl beh•beh_

For Eating Out, see page 150.

Disabled Travelers

Is there…?	**¿Hay…?** *aye…*
access for the disabled	**acceso para los discapacitados** *ahk·<u>seh</u>·soh <u>pah</u>·rah lohs dees·kah·pah·see·<u>tah</u>·dohs*
a wheelchair ramp	**una rampa para sillas de ruedas** *<u>oo</u>·nah <u>rahm</u>·pah <u>pah</u>·rah <u>see</u>·yahs deh <u>rweh</u>·dahs*
a handicapped [disabled] accessible toilet	**un baño con acceso para discapacitados** *oon <u>bah</u>·nyoh kohn ahk·<u>seh</u>·soh <u>pah</u>·rah dees·kah·pah·see·<u>tah</u>·dohs*
I need…	**Necesito…** *neh·seh·<u>see</u>·toh…*
assistance	**ayuda** *ah·<u>yoo</u>·dah*
an elevator [a lift]	**un ascensor** *oon ah·sehn·<u>sohr</u>*
a ground floor room	**una habitación en la planta baja** *<u>oo</u>·nah <u>oo</u>·nah ah·bee·tah·<u>seeyohn</u> ehn lah <u>plahn</u>·tah <u>bah</u>·khah*

Health & Emergencies

Emergencies

Help!	**¡Socorro!**	*soh·koh·rroh*
Go away!	**¡Váyase!**	*bah·yah·seh*
Stop, thief!	**¡Deténgase, ladrón!**	*deh·tehn·gah·seh lah·drohn*
Get a doctor!	**¡Llame a un médico!**	*yah·meh ah oon meh·dee·koh*
Fire!	**¡Fuego!**	*fweh·goh*
I'm lost.	**Me he perdido.**	*meh eh pehr·dee·doh*
Can you help me?	**¿Puede ayudarme?**	*pweh·deh ah·yoo·dahr·meh*

YOU MAY HEAR...

Rellene este formulario.
reh·yeh·neh ehs·teh fohr·mooh·lah·reeoh

Fill out this form.

Su documento de identidad, por favor.
*soo doh·koo·mehn·toh deh
ee·dehn·tee·dahd pohr fah·bohr*

Your identification,
please.

¿Cuándo/Dónde ocurrió?
kwahn·doh/dohn·deh oh·koo·rreeyoh

When/Where did it
happen?

¿Puede describirlo *m*/describirla *f*?
*pweh·deh dehs·kree·beer·loh/
dehs·kree·beer·lah*

What does he/she
look like?

Health

I'm sick.	**Me siento mal.** *meh seeyehn·toh mahl*
I need an English-speaking doctor.	**Necesito un médico que hable inglés.** *neh·seh·see·toh oon meh·dee·koh keh ah·bleh een·glehs*
It hurts here.	**Me duele aquí.** *meh dweh·leh ah·kee*
I have a stomachache.	**Tengo dolor de estómago.** *tehn·goh doh·lohr deh ehs·toh·mah·goh*
Where's the pharmacy [chemist]?	**¿Dónde está la farmacia?** *dohn·deh ehs·tah lah fahr·mah·seeyah*
I'm . . . (months) pregnant.	**Estoy embarazada de.... meses.** *ehs·toy ehm·bah·rah·sah·dah deh… meh·sehs*
I'm on...	**Estoy tomando...** *ehs·toy toh·mahn·doh…*
I'm allergic to antibiotics/penicillin.	**Soy alérgico m/alérgica f a los antibióticos/ la penicilina.** *soy ah·lehr·khee·koh/ah·lehr·khee·kah ah lohs ahn·tee·beeyoh·tee·kohs/lah peh·nee·see·lee·na*

Contact your consulate, ask the concierge at your hotel or ask the tourist information office for telephone numbers of the local ambulance, emergency services and police.

Dictionary

A

accident el accidente
accommodation el alojamiento
adapter el adaptador
address la dirección
after después; ~**noon** la tarde; ~**shave** la loción para después de afeitar
alone solo
ambulance la ambulancia
American estadounidense
anything algo
appointment la cita
ATM el cajero automático
attractive guapo

B

baby el bebé; ~ **bottle** el biberón; ~ **wipe** la toallita; ~**sitter** el/la niñero/a
back la espalda; ~**ache** el dolor de espalda; ~**pack** la mochila
bag la maleta
baggage el equipaje; ~ **claim** el reclamo de equipaje; ~ **ticket** el talón de equipaje
bakery la panadería
bank el banco
bar el bar
barber la peluquería de caballeros
bathroom el baño
be v ser/estar
beach la playa
beautiful precioso
bed la cama; ~ **and breakfast** la pensión

beginner principiante
behind detrás de
better mejor
bicycle la bicicleta
big grande
bird el pájaro
black negro
blue azul
board v embarcar
boat el barco
bottle la botella; **~ opener** el abrebotellas
boy el niño; **~friend** el novio
breakdown la avería
breakfast el desayuno
British británico
brother el hermano
brown marrón
bug el insecto
bus el autobús; **~ station** la estación de autobuses; **~ stop** la parada de
autobús; **~ ticket** el boleto de autobús; **~ tour** el recorrido en autobús
buy v comprar

C

cafe la cafetería
call v llamar; n la llamada
can opener el abrelatas
car el auto; **~ hire [BE]** el alquiler de autos; **~ park [BE]** el estacionamiento;
~ rental el alquiler de autos; **~ seat** el asiento de niño
cell phone el teléfono celular
change v **(buses)** cambiar; **~** n **(money)** el cambio
cheap barato

Cheers! ¡Salud!
chewing gum el chicle
child el niño; ~ **seat** la silla para niños
church la iglesia
cigar el puro
closed cerrado
clothing la ropa; ~ **store** la tienda de ropa
club la discoteca
coin la moneda
cold *n* **(sickness)** el resfriado; ~ **adj (temperature)** frío
conditioner el acondicionador
condom el preservativo
contact lens el lente de contacto; ~ **solution** el líquido de lentes de contacto
cook *v* cocinar
cool (temperature) frío
corkscrew el sacacorchos
cost *v* costar
cot el catre
cute bonito

D

dance *v* bailar; ~ **club** la discoteca
dangerous peligroso
day el día
deaf sordo
decline *v* **(credit card)** rechazar
degrees (temperature) los grados
delay *v* retrasarse
delicious delicioso
dentist el dentista
denture la dentadura

department store los grandes almacenes
departures (airport) las salidas
deposit *v* depositar; ~ *n* **(bank)** el depósito bancario; ~ *n* **(reserve a room)** la fianza
diabetic diabético
diaper el pañal
diarrhea la diarrea
difficult difícil
direction la dirección
dirty sucio
disabled discapacitado
discount el descuento
dish (kitchen) el plato; **~washer** el lavavajillas; **~washing liquid** el líquido lavavajillas
disposable desechable; ~ **razor** la cuchilla desechable
dive *v* bucear
diving equipment el equipo de buceo
dizzy mareado
doctor el médico
doll la muñeca
dollar (U.S.) el dólar
domestic nacional; ~ **flight** el vuelo nacional
door la puerta
double bed la cama matrimonial
downtown el centro
dress (piece of clothing) el vestido; ~ **code** las normas de vestuario
drink *v* beber; ~ *n* la bebida; ~ **menu** la carta de bebidas; **~ing water** el agua potable
drive *v* conducir
during durante
duty (tax) el impuesto; **~-free** libre de impuestos

E

early temprano
earrings los pendientes
east el este
easy fácil
eat *v* comer
electric outlet el enchufe eléctrico
e-mail *v* enviar un correo electrónico; ~ *n* el correo electrónico; ~ **address** la dirección de correo electrónico
emergency la emergencia; ~ **exit** la salida de emergencia
end *v* terminar
English el inglés
evening la noche
excess el exceso
exchange *v* **(money)** cambiar; ~ *v* **(goods)** devolver; ~ *n* **(place)** la casa de cambio; ~ **rate** el tipo de cambio
excuse *v* **(to get past)** pedir perdón; ~ *v* **(to get attention)** disculparse
exhausted agotado
exit *v* salir; ~ *n* la salida
expensive caro
extra adicional; ~ **large** equis ele **(XL)**

F

family la familia
fan (appliance) el ventilador; ~ **(souvenir)** el abanico
far lejos; ~**-sighted** hipermétrope
fast rápido; ~ **food** la comida rápida
faster más rápido
father el padre
food la comida
football [BE] el fútbol

for para/por
fork el tenedor
formula (baby) la fórmula infantil
free gratuito
friend el amigo
full completo; **~-service** el servicio completo; **~-time** a tiempo completo

G

get to v ir a
get off v **(a train/bus/subway)** bajarse
gift el regalo; **~ shop** la tienda de regalos
girl la niña; **~friend** la novia
give v dar
glass (drinking) el vaso; **~ (material)** el vidrio
glasses las gafas
go v **(somewhere)** ir a
gold el oro
golf golf; **~ course** el campo de golf; **~ tournament** el torneo de golf
good n el producto; **~** adj bueno; **~ afternoon** buenas tardes; **~ evening** buenas noches; **~ morning** buenos días; **~bye** adiós
grandparent el abuelo
gray gris
green verde
guide el guía; **~ book** la guía; **~ dog** el perro guía

H

hair el pelo; **~ dryer** el secador de pelo; **~ salon** la peluquería; **~brush** el cepillo de pelo; **~cut** el corte de pelo; **~spray** la laca; **~style** el peinado
half medio; **~ hour** la media hora; **~-kilo** el medio kilo
hand la mano; **~ luggage [BE]** el equipaje de mano; **~bag [BE]** el bolso
handicapped discapacitado
hangover la resaca

happy feliz
hat el sombrero
have v tener
heat v calentar; ~ n el calor
help v ayudar; ~ n la ayuda
here aquí
hire v [BE] alquilar; ~ **car** [BE] el coche de alquiler
hospital el hospital
hot (temperature) caliente; ~ **(spicy)** picante; ~ **spring** el agua termal;
  ~ **water** el agua caliente
hour la hora
how (question) cómo; ~ **much (question)** cuánto cuesta
husband el marido

I

identification el documento de identidad
insect el insecto; ~ **bite** la picadura de insecto; ~ **repellent** el repelente de
  insectos
insurance el seguro
interesting interesante
internet la internet; ~ **cafe** el cibercafé; ~ **service** el servicio de internet;
  wireless ~ el acceso inalámbrico
Ireland Irlanda
Irish irlandés

J

jacket la chaqueta
jar el bote
jaw la mandíbula
jazz el jazz; ~ **club** el club de jazz
jeans los vaqueros
jet ski la moto acuática

jeweler la joyería
join *v* acompañar a
joint (body part) la articulación

K

key la llave; ~ **card** la llave electrónica; ~ **ring** el llavero
kiddie pool la piscina infantil
kiss *v* besar
kitchen la cocina; ~ **foil [BE]** el papel de aluminio
knee la rodilla
knife el cuchillo

L

lactose intolerant intolerante a la lactosa
large grande; ~**er** más grande
last último
late (time) tarde; ~er más tarde
launderette [BE] la lavandería
lawyer el abogado
leather el cuero
to leave *v* salir
left (direction) la izquierda
less menos
lesson la lección
lighter el encendedor
like *v* gustar; **I like** me gusta
lip el labio
liquor store la tienda de bebidas alcohólicas
little pequeño
live *v* vivir
lock *v* cerrar; ~ *n* el cerrojo
log on *v* **(computer)** iniciar sesión

log off *v* **(computer)** cerrar sesión

long largo; ~ **sleeves** las mangas largas; ~-**sighted [BE]** hipermétrope

look *v* mirar

lose *v* **(something)** perder

lost perdido; ~ **and found** la oficina de objetos perdidos

love *v* querer; ~ *n* el amor

low bajo; ~**er** más bajo

luggage el equipaje; ~ **cart** el carrito de equipaje; ~ **locker** el casillero automático; ~ **ticket** el talón de equipaje; **hand** ~ **[BE]** el equipaje de mano

lunch la comida

M

magazine la revista

mall el centro comercial

man el hombre

manager el gerente

map el mapa

market el mercado

mass (church service) la misa

massage el masaje

match el fósforo

meal la comida

measure *v* **(someone)** medir

medicine el medicamento

menstrual cramps los dolores menstruales

message el mensaje

midday [BE] el mediodía

midnight la medianoche

missing desaparecido

mistake el error

mobile móvil; **~ home** la caravana; **~ phone [BE]** el teléfono celular
money el dinero
month el mes
moped el ciclomotor
more más
morning la mañana
mosque la mezquita
mother la madre
motion sickness el mareo
museum el museo
music la música

N

nail la u~na; **~ file** la lima de uñas; **~ salon** el salón de manicura
name el nombre
nappy [BE] el pañal
(be) nauseous *v* tener náuseas
near cerca; **~-sighted** miope; **~by** cerca de aquí
necklace el collar
need *v* necesitar
newspaper el periódico
next próximo
nice amable
night la noche; **~club** la discoteca
no no
north el norte
nothing nada
now ahora
number el número
nurse el enfermero/la enfermera

O

office la oficina; ~ **hours (doctor's)** las horas de consulta; ~ **hours (other offices)** el horario de oficina
off-licence [BE] la tienda de bebidas alcohólicas
OK de acuerdo
old viejo
once una vez
one uno; ~**-way ticket** el billete de ida; ~**-way street** la calle de sentido único
only solamente
open v abrir; ~ *adj* abierto
opposite frente a
optician el oculista
orange (color) naranja
order v pedir
outside fuera
over sobre; ~ **the counter (medication)** sin receta; ~**look (scenic place)** el mirador; ~**night** por la noche

P

pacifier el chupete
pack v hacer las maletas
pain el dolor
pants los pantalones
paper el papel; ~ **towel** el papel de cocina
park v aparcar; ~n el parque; ~**ing garage** el párking; ~**ing lot** el estacionamiento
passport el pasaporte; ~ **control** el control de pasaportes
pay v pagar; ~ **phone** el teléfono público
pen el bolígrafo
per por; ~ **day** por día; ~ **hour** por hora; ~ **night** por noche; ~ **week** por semana

period (menstrual) la regla; ~ (of time) la época
petrol la gasolina; **~ station** la gasolinera
pharmacy la farmacia
phone *v* hacer una llamada; **~** *n* el teléfono; **~ call** la llamada de teléfono; **~ card** la tarjeta telefónica; **~ number** el número de teléfono
photo la foto; **~copy** la fotocopia; **~graphy** la fotografía
pill (birth control) la píldora
pink rosa
plane el avión
plate el plato
play *v* jugar; **~** *n* **(theater)** la obra de teatro; **~ground** el patio de recreo; **~pen** el parque
please por favor
police la policía; **~ report** el certificado de la policía; **~ station** la comisaría
pool la piscina
pounds (British sterling) las libras esterlinas
pregnant embarazada
prescription la receta
press *v* **(clothing)** planchar
price el precio
print *v* imprimir
problem el problema
purple morado
purse el bolso
push *v* **(door sign)** empujar; **~chair [BE]** el coche de niño

Q

quality la calidad
question la pregunta
quiet tranquilo

R

racket (sports) la raqueta

rain la lluvia; **~coat** el chubasquero; **~forest** el bosque pluvial; **~y** lluvioso

rape *v* violar; *~ n* la violación

rash la erupción cutánea

reach *v* localizar

ready listo

real auténtico

receipt el recibo

recharge v recargar

recommend v recomendar

red rojo

reservation la reserva; **~ desk** la taquilla

restroom el servicio

return *v* **(something)** devolver; *~ n* **[BE]** la ida y vuelta

right (direction) derecha; **~ of way** prioridad de paso

room la habitación; **~ key** la llave de habitación; **~ service** el servicio de habitaciones

round-trip ida y vuelta

S

sad triste

same mismo

sanitary napkin la toalla higiénica

scanner el escáner

scissors las tijeras

sea el mar

see *v* ver

self-service el autoservicio

shampoo el champú

shirt la camisa

shoe store la zapatería

shopping ir de compras; ~ **area** la zona de compras; ~ **centre [BE]** el centro comercial; ~ **mall** el centro comercial

short corto

shower la ducha

sick enfermo

single (unmarried) soltero; ~ **bed** la cama; ~ **prints** una copia; ~ **room** una habitación individual

sink el lavabo

sister la hermana

sit v sentarse

size la talla

sleep v dormir; ~**er car** el coche cama; ~**ing bag** el saco de dormir

slowly despacio

small pequeño

smoke v fumar

soccer el fútbol

sock el calcetín

some alguno

soother [BE] el chupete

sore throat las anginas

sorry lo siento

south el sur

souvenir el recuerdo; ~ **store** la tienda de recuerdos

spa el centro de salud y belleza

Spain España

Spanish el español

speak v hablar

spell v deletrear

spicy picante

station la estación; **bus** ~ la estación de autobuses; **gas** ~ la gasolinera;
   muster ~ **[BE]** el punto de reunión; **petrol** ~ **[BE]** la gasolinera;
   subway ~ el metro; **train** ~ la estación de tren
stay *v* quedarse
stomach el estómago; **~ache** el dolor de estómago
stop *v* pararse; ~ *n* la parada
straight recto
stroller el coche
student el estudiante
suitcase la maleta
sun el sol; **~block** el protector solar total; **~burn** la quemadura solar;
   ~glasses las gafas de sol; **~ny** soleado; **~screen** el protector solar;
   ~stroke la insolación

T

table la mesa
take *v* llevar; ~ **away [BE]** para llevar
tampon el tampón
text *v* **(send a message)** enviar un mensaje de texto; ~ *n* **(message)** el texto
thank *v* dar las gracias a; ~ **you** gracias
that eso
thirsty sediento
this esto
ticket el boleto; ~ **office** el despacho de boletos; **~ed passenger** el pasajero
   con boleto
tie (clothing) la corbata
time el tiempo; **~table [BE]** el horario
tired cansado
tissue el pañuelo de papel
today hoy
toilet [BE] el servicio; ~ **paper** el papel higiénico

tomorrow mañana
tongue la lengua
tonight esta noche
too demasiado
tooth el diente; **~brush** el cepillo de dientes; **~paste** la pasta de dientes
total (amount) el total
tough (food) duro
towel la toalla
train el tren; **~ station** la estación de tren
translate *v* traducir
trip el viaje

U

United Kingdom (U.K.) el Reino Unido
United States (U.S.) los Estados Unidos
ugly feo
umbrella el paraguas

V

vacancy la habitación libre
vacation las vacaciones
vaccination la vacuna
village el pueblo
vineyard la viña
visit *v* visitar; **~ing hours** el horario de visita
vomit *v* vomitar

W

wait *v* esperar; **~** *n* la espera; **~ing room** la sala de espera
waiter el camarero; **waitress** la camarera
wake *v* despertarse; **~-up call** la llamada despertador
walk *v* caminar; **~** *n* la caminata; **~ing route** la ruta de senderismo

wallet la cartera
weather el tiempo
week la semana; ~**end** el fin de semana; ~**ly** semanal
welcome *v* acoger; ~ bienvenido
well bien; ~**-rested** descansado
west el oeste
what (question) qué
wheelchair la silla de ruedas; ~ **ramp** la rampa para silla de ruedas
when (question) cuándo
where (question) dónde
white blanco; ~ **gold** el oro blanco
wife la mujer
wireless inalámbrico; ~ **internet** el acceso inalámbrico a internet;
with con
without sin
woman la mujer
work *v* trabajar

Y

year el año
yellow amarillo; ~ **gold** el oro amarillo
yes sí
yesterday ayer
young joven
youth hostel el albergue juvenil

Z

zoo el zoológico

Quechua

Essentials

Hello/Hi.	**Imaynalla/Tuy.**	*Ee-mah-ee-nah-yah/Tooy*
Goodbye.	**Tinkunakama.**	*Teen-koo-nah-kah-mah*
Yes/No/Okay.	**Ari/Mana/Allimi.**	*Ah-ree/Mah-nah/Ah-yee-mee*
Excuse me! (to get attention)	**¡Qhispichiway!**	*Kees-pee-chee-wahy*
Excuse me. (to get past)	**¡Panpanchaway!**	*Pahn-pahn-chah-wahy*
I'm sorry.	**Qhispichiwaylla.**	*Kees-pee-chee-wahy-yah*
I'd like…	**Munani…**	*Moo-nah-nee*
How much?	**¿Machkha chaniyuq?**	*Mah-chkah chah-nee-yohk*
And/or.	**Chaymanta/utaq.**	*Chahy-mahn-tah/oo-tahk*
Please.	**Ama hina kay.**	*Ah-mah khee-nah kahy*
Thank you.	**Pachi.**	*Pah-chee*
You're welcome.	**Allillan hamunki.**	*Ahyee-yahn ah-moon-kee*
Where's…?	**¿Maypi …kanchu?**	*Mahy-pee … kahn-choo*
I'm going to…	**Kay … richkanki.**	*Kahy … ree-chkah-nkee*
My name is…	**… sutini.**	*… soo-tee-nee*
Please speak slowly.	**Allillamanta parlarikun.**	*Ah-yee-yah-mahn-tah pahr-lah-ree-koon*
Can you repeat that?	**¿Kayta watiqmanta niy atikunkichu?**	*Kahy-tah wah-tehk-mahn-tah neey ah-tee-koon-kee-choo*
I don't understand.	**Mana yachanichu.**	*Mah-nah yah-chah-nee-choo*
Do you speak English?	**¿Inglés simipi parlankichu?**	*Een-glehs see-mee-pee pahr-ahn-kee-choo*
I don't speak (much) Quechua.	**Mana (achka) Quechua parlanichu.**	*Mah-nah (ahch-kah) Quechua pahr-lah-nee-choo*
Where's the restroom [toilet]?	**¿Maypi hisp'ana [jisp'ana] k'uchu kachkan?**	*Mahy-pee khees-pah-nah [khees-pah-nah] koo-choo kah-chkahn*
Help!	**¡Yanapay!**	*Yah-nah-pahy*

Numbers

0	**cero** *theh·roh*
1	**huk** *khook*
2	**iskay** *ees·kahy*
3	**kimsa** *keem·sah*
4	**tawa** *tah·wah*
5	**phisqa** *pees·kaa*
6	**suqta** *sohk·tah*
7	**qanchis** *kahn·chees*
8	**pusaq** *poo·sahk*
9	**isqun** *ees·kohn*
10	**chunka** *choon·kah*
11	**chunka hukniyuq** *choon·kah khook·nee·yohk*
12	**chunka iskayniyuq** *choon·kah ees·kahy·nee·yohk*
13	**chunka kimsayuq** *choon·kah keem·sah·yohk*
14	**chunka tawayuq** *choon·kah tah·wah·yohk*
15	**chunka phisqayuq** *choon·kah pees·kah·yohk*
16	**chunka suqtayuq** *choon·kah sohk·tah·yohk*

You'll find the pronunciation of the Quechua letters and words written in gray after each sentence to guide you. Simply pronounce these as if they were English. As you hear the language being spoken, you will quickly become accustomed to the local pronunciation and dialect.

Quechua or 'the people's language' as it is often referred to, is spoken primarily in the Andes. You'll come across it in Argentina, Bolivia, Colombia, Ecuador and Peru. There are an estimated 8 to 10 million speakers.

17	**chunka qanchisniyuq** *choon·kah kahn·chees·nee·yohk*
18	**chunka pusaqniyuq** *choon·kah poo·sahk·nee·yook*
19	**chunka isqunniyuq** *choon·kah ees·kohn·nee·yohk*
20	**iskay chunka** *ees·kahy choon·kah*
21	**iskay chunka hukniyuq** *ees·kahy choon·kah khook·nee·yohk*
30	**kimsa chunka** *keem·sah choon·kah*
40	**tawa chunka** *tah·wah choon·kah*
50	**phisqa chunka** *pees·kah choon·kah*
60	**suqta chunka** *sohk·tah choon·kah*
70	**qanchis chunka** *kahn·chees choon·kah*
80	**pusaq chunka** *poo·sahk choon·kah*
90	**isqun chunka** *ees·kohn choon·kah*
100	**one hundred** *pachaq pah·chahk*
101	**pachaq hukniyuq** *pah·chahk khuk·nee·yohk*
200	**pachaq iskayniyuq** *pah·chahk ees·kahy·nee·yohk*
500	**pachaq phisqaniyuq** *pah·chahk pees·kah·nee·yohk*
1,000	**huk hunu** *khuk oo·noo*
10,000	**chunka hunu** *choon·kah oo·noo*
1,000,000	**waranqa** *wah·rahn·kah*

Time

What time is it?	**¿Ima pachata kanchu?** *Ee·mah pah·chah·tah kahn·choo*
It's midday.	**Kuskhan punchaw kan.** *Koos·kahn poon·chahw kahn*
Five past three.	**Phisqa pacha chunka kimsaniyuq chinini.** *Pees·kah pah·chah choon·kah keem·sah·nee·yohk chee·nee·nee*
A quarter to ten.	**Isqun pacha tawa chunka phisqaniyuq chinini.** *Ees·kohn pah·chah tah·wah choon·kah pees·kah·nee·yohk chee·nee·nee*
5:30 a.m./p.m.	**5:30 a.m./p.m.** *pees·kah pah·chah keem·sah chee·nee·nee ah·eh·meh/peh·eh·meh*

Days

Monday	**Killachaw**	*Kee·yah·chahw*
Tuesday	**Atipachaw**	*Ah·tee·pah·chahw*
Wednesday	**Quyllurchaw**	*Kooy·yoor·chahw*
Thursday	**Ch' askachaw**	*Chahs·kah·chahw*
Friday	**Illapachaw**	*Ee·yah·pah·chahw*
Saturday	**K'uychichaw**	*Kooy·chee·chahw*
Sunday	**Intichaw**	*Een·tee·chahw*

Dates

yesterday	**qayna punchaw** *kahy·nah poon·chahw*
today	**kunan punchaw** *koo·nahn poon·chahw*
tomorrow	**paqarin punchaw** *pah·kah·reen poon·chahw*
day	**punchaw** *poon·chahw*
week	**qanchischaw** *kahn·chees·chahw*
month	**killa** *kee·yah*
year	**wata** *wah·tah*
Happy New Year!	**¡Kusi Musuq Watayuq!** *Koo·see Moo·suuk Wah·tah·yohk*
Happy Birthday!	**¡Kusi Wata Punchawniyuq!** *Koo·see Wah·tah Poon·chahw·nee·yohk*

Months

January	**Qulla puquy** *Koo·yah poh·kohy*
February	**Hatun puquy** *Khah·toon poh·kohy*
March	**Pauqar waray** *Pahw·kahr wah·rahy*
April	**Ayriwa** *Ay·ree·wah*
May	**Aymuray** *Ay·moo·rahy*
June	**Inti raymi** *Een·tee rahy·mee*
July	**Anta Sitwa** *Ahn·tah Seet·wah*

August	**Qhapaq Sitwa** *Kah·pahk Seet·wah*
September	**Uma raymi** *Oo·mah rahy·mee*
October	**Kantaray** *Kahn·tah·rahy*
November	**Ayamarq'a** *Ahyah·mahr·kah*
December	**Kapaq Raymi** *Kah·pahk Rahy·mee*

Arrival & Departure

I'm on vacation [holiday]/business.	**Samanapi [hatun punchawpi]/llamkanapi kani.** *Sah·mah·nah·pee [ah·toon poon·chahw·pee]/ yahm·kah·nah·pee kah·nee*
I'm going to...	**... kaqman richkani** *... kahk·mahn ree·chkah·nee*
I'm staying at the...Hotel.	**... Puñuna wasipi** *... Poo·ñoo·nah wah·see·pee* **kachkani.** *kah·chkah·nee*

Money

Where's...?	**¿Maypi ... kanchu?** *Mahy·pee ... kahn·choo*
the ATM	**ATM nisqata** *ATM nees·kah·tah*
the bank	**banco nisqata** *bahn·koo nees·kah·tah*
the currency exchange office	**qullqip tikraynin kitita** *Kohl·keh teek·rahy·neen kee·tee·tah*
When does the bank open/close?	**¿Imay pacha banco kichayta/wichq'ayta kanchu?** *Ee·mahy pah·chah bahn·koo kee·chahy·tah/ wee·chkahy·tah kahn·choo*
I'd like to change pounds sterling/ euros into dollars.	**Libra esterlina/euros dolar kaqman tikray munani.** *lee·brah ees·teer·lee·nah/ehw·rohs doo·lahr kahk·mahn teek·rahy moo·nah·nee*
I'd like to cash traveler's cheques.	**Puriqpa chequekunan munani.** *Poo·reek·pah cheh·keh·koo·nahn moo·nah·nee*
Can I pay in cash?	**¿Qullqiwan paypay atikunichu?** *Kohl·keh·wahn pahy·pahy ah·tee·koo·nee·choo*

Can I pay by (credit) card?	¿(manukuy) tarjetawan paypay atikunichu? *(mah•noo•kooy) tahr•kheh•tah•wahn pahy•pahy ah•tee•koo•nee•choo*

Getting Around

How do I get to town?	¿Imaynataq llaqtaman rini? *eemah•ynah•tahk llahk•tah•mahn ree•nee?*
Where's…?	¿Maypi… kanchu? *Mahy•pee … kahn•choo*
the airport	aeropuertota *ah•eh•roh•pwehr•toh•tah*
the train station	estacion trenpaq *ehs•tah•thee•ohn trehn•pahk*
the bus station	estacion buspaq *ehs•tah•zee•ohn boos•pahk*
the subway [underground] station	subteraneota [metrota] estacion *soob•teh•rrah•nehw•tah [meh•troh•tah] ehs•tah•thee•ohn*
Is it far from here?	¿Karu kaypimanta kanchu? *Kah•roo kahy•pee•mahn•tah kahn•choo*
Where do I buy a ticket?	¿Maypi huk boleto rantiy kanichu? *Mahy•pee khook boh•leh•toh rahn•teey kah•nee•choo*
A one-way/ return-trip ticket to…	Huk boleto riypaq/kutiypaq …kaqman. *Khook boh•leh•toh reey•pahk/koo•teey•pahk … kahk•mahn*

195

YOU MAY HEAR...

chiqan *cheh·kahn*	straight ahead
lluq'i *yoh·keh*	left
paña *pah·nyah*	right
k'uchu muyuyrayku *koo·choo moo·yooy·rahy·koo*	around the corner
ayñi *ahy·nyee*	opposite
qhipallanta *keh·pah·yahn·tah*	behind
qatiq *kah·teek*	next to
chanta *chahn·tah*	after
chincha/urin *cheen·chah/oo·reen*	north/south
anti/kunti *ahn·tee/koon·tee*	east/west
trafico illata *trah·fee·koo ee·yah·tah*	at the traffic light
intersecciona *een·tehr·seh·xee·ohn·tah*	at the intersection

How much?	**¿Machka chaniyuq?** *Mah·chkah chah·nee·yohk*
Which gate/line?	**¿Ima punku/sinri?** *Ee·mah poon·koo/seen·ree*
Which platform?	**¿Ima plataforma?** *Ee·mah plah·tah·foor·mah*
Where can I get a taxi?	**¿Maypi huk taxi tariyta atikunichu?** *Mahy·pee khook tah·xee tah·reey·tah ah·thee·koo·nee·choo*
Take me to this address.	**Kay tarikuqman apaway.** *Kahy tah·ree·kook·mahn ah·pah·wahy*
To...Airport, please.	**...aeropuertoman, ama hina kay.** *...ah·eh·roh·pwehr·toh·mahn ah·mah khi·nah kahy*
I'm in a rush.	**Usqhaqwan kani.** *Oos·kahk·wahn kah·nee*
Can I have a map?	**¿Huk mapa tiyayta atikunichu?** *Khook mah·pah teey·ahy·tah ah·tee·koo·nee·choo*

For Numbers, see page 190.

Tickets

When's…to Cusco?	**¿Imay pacha … Qosqo kaqman kanchu?** *Eemahy pah·chah … coz·coh kahk·mahn kahn·choo*
the (first) bus	**(hukñiqi) bus** *(khook·nyee·keh) boos*
the (next) flight	**(qatiq) vuelo** *(kah·teek) bweh·loo*
the (last) train	**(qhipa) tren** *(keh·pah) trehn*
One/Two ticket(s) please.	**Huk/Iskay boleto(kuna).** *Khook/Ees·kahy boh·eh·toh(koo·nah)*
For today/tomorrow.	**Kunan punchawpaq/paqarin punchawpaq.** *Koo·nahn poon·chahw·pahk/pah·kah·reen poon·chahw·pahk*
A…ticket.	**Huk…boleto.** *Khook… boh·leh·toh*
one-way	**riypaq** *reey·pahk*
return trip	**kutiypaq rina** *koo·teey·pahk ree·nah*
first class	**hukñiqin clase** *khook·nyee·keen clah·seh*
I have an e-ticket.	**Huk boleto electronico tiyani.** *Khook boh·leh·toh eh·lehk·troh·nee·koo tee·yah·nee*
How long is the trip?	**¿Imay pacha rinata kanchu?** *Ee·mahy pah·chah ree·nah·tah kahn·choo*
Is it a direct train?	**¿Chiqan tren kanchu?** *Cheh·kahn trehn kahn·choo*
Is this the bus to…?	**¿Kay bus … kaqman kanchu?** *Kahy boos … kahk·mahn kahn·choo*
Can you tell me when to get off?	**¿Niway maypi uraykachiy tiyanichu?** *Nee·wahy mahy·pee oo·rahy·kah·cheey tee·yah·nee·choo*
I'd like to… my reservation.	**… kaqman munani waqaychanay.** *… kahk·mahn moo·nah·nee wah·kahy·chah·nahy*
cancel	**chinkachiy** *cheen·kah·cheey*
change	**tikray** *teek·rahy*
confirm	**uyakuy** *oo·yah·kooy*

For Time, see page 192.

Car Hire

Where's the car hire?	**¿Maypi auto alkilaypaq kanchu?** *Mahy·pee ahw·too ahl·kee·lahy·pahk kahn·schoo*
I'd like…	**… munani** *… moo·nah·nee*
a cheap/small car	**huk barato/huchuy auto** *khook bah·rah·too/oo·chooy ahw·too*
an automatic/ a manual	**huk automatico/huk manual** *khook* *ahw·too·mah·tee·koo/khook mah·noo·ahl*
air conditioning	**acondicionado wayra** *ah·koon·dee·zee·oh·nah·doh*
a car seat	**huk tiyana automanta** *khook tee·yah·nah* *ahw·toh·mahn·tah*
How much…?	**¿Machka chaniyuq…?** *Mah·chkah chah·nee·yohk*
per day/week	**sapa punchaw/qanchischaw** *sah·pah poon·chahw/kahn·chees·chahw*
Are there any discounts?	**¿Wakin pisi qullqi kankuchu?** *Wah·keen pee·see* *kohl·keh kahn·koo·choo*

Places to Stay

Can you recommend a hotel?	**¿Huk puñuna wasi niy atikunkichu?** *Khook poo·nyoo·nah wah·see neey ah·tee·koon·kee·choo*
I made a reservation.	**Huk waqaychana ruwani.** *Khook wah·kahy·chah·nah roo·wah·nee*
My name is...	**... sutiy kani** *... soo·teey kah·nee*
Do you have a room...?	**¿Huk cuarto tiyayta kankichu?** *Khook koo·ahr·too tee·yahy·tah kahn·kee·choo*
for one/two	**huk runapaq/iskay runapaq** *khook roo·nah-pahk/ ees·kahk roo·nah·pahk*
with a bathroom	**huk bañowan** *khook bah·nyoo·wahn*
with air conditioning	**acondicionado wayrawan** *ah·koon·dee·thee·oh·nah·doh wahy·rah·wahn*
For...	**Kay...** *Kahy ...*
tonight	**kunan tutapaq** *koo·nahn too·tah·pahk*
two nights	**iskay tutapaq** *ees·kahy too·tah·pahk*
one week	**huk qanchischawpaq** *khok kahn·chees·chahw·pahk*
How much?	**¿Machka chaniyuq?** *Mah·chkah chah·nee·yohk*
Is there anything cheaper?	**¿Wakin barato imata kanchu?** *Wah·keen bah·rah·too ee·mah·tah kahn·choo*

When's checkout?	**¿Imay pacha waqaychay kanchu?** *Ee•mahy pah•chah wah•kahy•chahy kahn•choo*
Can I leave this in the safe?	**¿Kay ima caja fuertepi usachikuy atikunichu?** *Kahy ee•mah kah•khah fwehr•teh•pee oo•sah•chee•kooy ah•tee•koo•nee•choo*
Can I leave my bags?	**¿Maletakunay usachikuy atikunichu?** *Mah•leh•tah•koo•nahy oo•sah•chee•kooy ah•tee•koo•nee•choo*
Can I have my bill/ a receipt?	**¿Boletoy/huk reciboy usachikuy atikunichu?** *Boh•leh•tooy/khook reh•thee•bohy oo•sah•chee•kooy ah•tee•koo•nee•choo*
I'll pay in cash/ by credit card.	**Qullqiwan/manukuy tarjetawan payllani.** *Kohy•keh•wahn/mah•noo•kooy tahr•kheh•tah•wahn pahy•yah•nee*

Communications

Where's an internet cafe?	**¿Maypi huk café internetpi kanchu?** *Mahy•pee khook kah•feh een•teer•neet•pee kahn•choo*
Can I access the internet/check my email?	**¿Internetman yaykuy/correo electronicoy chiqaqchay atikunichu?** *Een•teer•neet•mahn yahy•kooy/koh•rreh•woh eh•lehc•troh•nee•cohy chehk•ahk•chahy*
How much per half hour/hour?	**¿Machka sapa kuska horata/huk horata kanchu?** *Mah•chkah sah•pah koos•kah oo•rah•tah/khook oo•rah•tah kahn•choo*
How do I connect/ log on?	**¿Imayna tinkini/llamkay qallanini?** *Ee•mahy•nah teen•kee•nee/yahm•kahy ka•ya•nee•nee*
A phone card, please.	**Huk tarjeta telefonopaq, ama hina kay.** *Khook tahr•kheh•tah thee•lee•foo•noo•pahk ah•mah ee•nah kahy*

Can I have your phone number?	**¿Telefono yupayniy tiyay atikunichu?** *Tee·lee·foo·noo yoo·pahy·neey tee·yahy ah·tee·koo·nee·choo*
Here's my number/email.	**Kaypi yupayniy/correo electronicoy kan.** *Kahy·pee yoo·pahy·neey/coh·rreh·oh eh·lehk·troo·nee·kuuy kahn*
Call me/text me.	**Qawaway/huk SMS apachiway.** *Kah·wah·wahy/khook Eh·seh Eh·meh Eh·seh ah·pah·chee·wahy*
I'll text you.	**Huk SMS apachini.** *Khuk Eh·seh Eh·meh Eh·seh ah·pah·chee·nee*
Email me.	**Correo electronico apachiwayni.** *Coh·rreh·oh eh·lehk·troo·nee·kuu ah·pah·chee·wahy·nee*
Hello. This is…	**Imaynalla. Kayta … kan** *Ee·mahy·nah·yah. Kahy·tah … kahn*
Can I speak to…?	**¿… kaqman parlay atikunichu?** *… kahk·mahn pahr·lahy ah·tee·koo·nee·choo*
Can you repeat that?	**¿Kayta kutichiy atikunkichu?** *Kahy·tah koo·tee·cheey ah·tee·koon·kee·choo*
I'll call back later.	**Watiqmanta aswan qhipaman qayani.** *Wah·teek·mahn·tah ahs·wahn keh·pah·mahn kah·yah·nee*
Bye.	**Tinkunakama.** *Teen·koo·nah·kah·mah*

Where's the post office?	**¿Maypi postal oficina kanchu?** *Mahy·pee pohs·tahl oo·fee·thee·nah kahn·choo*
I'd like to send this to…	**Kayta … kaqman apachiy munani.** *Kahy·tah … kahk·mahn ah·pah·cheey moo·nah·nee*
Can I…?	**¿… atikunichu?** *… ah·tee·koo·nee·choo*
access the internet	**Internetman yaykuy** *Een·teer·neet·mahn yahy·kooy*
check my email	**Correo electronicoyman chiqaqchay** *Koo·rreh·oh eh·lehk·troh·nee·kooy·mahn cheh·kahk·chahy*
print	**Imprimiyta** *Eem·pree·meey·tah*
plug in/charge my laptop/iPhone/ iPad/BlackBerry?	**¿Computadoray/iPhone/iPad/BlackBerry qipichiy/tinkiy kanichu?** *Kohm·poo·tah·dooh·rahy/ ahy·fohn/ahy·pahd/blahk·beh·rree keh·pee·cheey teen·keey kah·nee·choo*
access Skype?	**¿Skype yaykuy?** *Ehs·kahy·peh yahy·kooy*
What is the WiFi password?	**¿Maypi WiFi kichanata kanchu?** *Mahy·pee Wahy·Fahy kee·chah·nah·tah kahn·choo*
Is the WiFi free?	**¿Qhasi WiFi kanchu?** *Kah·see Wahy·Fahy kahn·choo*
Do you have bluetooth?	**¿Bluetooth tiyanichu?** *Bloo·too tee·yah·nee·choo*
Do you have a scanner?	**¿Huk escanerta tiyanichu?** *Khuk ees·kah·ehr·tah tee·yah·nee·choo*

202

Social Media

Are you on Facebook/Twitter?	**¿ Facebook/Twitter nisqapi kanchu?** *Fah-thees-book/Too-ee-tehr nees-kah-pee kahn-choo*
What's your username?	**¿Ima ruwaq sutiyki kankichu?** *Ee-mah roo-wahk soo-teey-kee kahn-kee-choo*
I'll add you as a friend.	**Qamman masihina yapani.** *Kahm-mahn mah-see-khee-nah yah-pah-nee*
I'll follow you on Twitter.	**Qamta Twitter nisqapi qatini.** *Kahm-tah Too-ee-tehr nees-kah-pee kah-tee-nee*
Are you following...?	**¿... qatichkan kankichu?** *... kah-teech-kahn kahn-kee-choo*
I'll put the pictures on Facebook/Twitter.	**Fotokuna Facebook/Twitter nisqapi churani.** *Foh-toh-koo-nah Fah-thees-book/Too-ee-tehr nees-kah-pee choo-rah-nee*
I'll tag you in the pictures.	**Fotokunapi qamta etiqueta churani.** *Foh-toh-koo-nah-pee kahm-tah eh-tee-keh-tah choo-rah-nee*

Conversation

Hello!/Hi!	**¡Imaynalla/Tuy!** *Ee-mahee-nah-yah/Tooy*
How are you?	**¿Allillanchu?** *Ah-yee-yahn-choo*
Fine, thanks.	**Allillan, pachi** *Ah-yee-yahn, pah-chee*
Excuse me!	**¡Qhispichiwayku!** *Kees-pee-chee-wahy-koo*
Do you speak English?	**¿Ingles simita parlankichu?** *Een-glees see-mee-tah pahr-lahn-kee-choo*
What's your name?	**¿Ima sutinki?** *Ee-mah soo-teen-kee*
My name is...	**Sutiy...** *Soo-teey...*
Nice to meet you.	**Ancha reqsichikunki.** *Ahn-chah reek-see-chee-koon-kee*
Where are you from?	**¿Maymanta kanki?** *Mahy-mahn-tah kahn-kee*

I'm from the U.K./U.S.	**U.K./U.S nisqamanta kani.** *Reh·ee·noo Oo·nee·doo/ Ehs·tah·dohs Oo·nee·doos nees·qah·mahn·tah kah·nee*
What do you do for a living?	**¿Maypi llamkanki?** *Mahy·pee yahm·kahn·kee*
I work for. . .	**. . . nisqawan llamkani.** *. . . nees·ka·wahn yahm·kah·nee*
I'm a student.	**Yachakuq kani.** *Yah·chah·kook kah·nee*
I'm retired.	**Retirasqa kani.** *Reh·tee·rahs·ka kah·nee*

Romance

Would you like to go out for a drink/dinner?	**¿Huk upyanata/mikhunata munanki?** *Khuk oop·yah·nah·tah/mee·koo·nah·tah moo·nahn·kee*
What are your plans for tonight/tomorrow?	**¿Imataq kunan tuta/paqarin punchaw ruwanki?** *Ee·mah·tahk koo·nahn too·tah/pah·kah·reen poon·chahw roo·wahn·kee*
Can I have your (phone) number?	**¿(telefono) yupayniyki tiyay atikunichu?** *(tee·lee·foo·noo) yoo·pahy·neey·kee teey·hay ah·tee·koo·nee·choo*
Can I join you?	**¿Qamwan huñuykunakuy atikunichu?** *Kahm·wahn hoo·nyuy·koo·nah·kooy ah·tee·koo·nee·choo*

Can I buy you a drink?	**¿Huk upyana rantiy atikunichu?**
	Khook•oop•yah•nah rahn•teey ah•tee•koo•nee•choo
I love you.	**Qamta munanki.** *Kahm•tah moo•nahn•kee*

Accepting & Rejecting

I'd love to.	**Nuqapis munanki.**
	Noo•kah•pees moo•nahn•kee
Where should we meet?	**¿Maypi huñuykuchu?** *Mahy•pee hoo•nyuy•koo•choo*
I'll meet you at the bar/your hotel.	**Barpi/puñuna wasiykipi qamta huñuni.**
	Bar•pee/poo•nyoo•nah wah•seey•kee•pee qahm•tah hoo•nyoo•nee
I'll come by at…	**… pachapi yachakamuni.** … *pah•chah•pee yah•chah•kah•moo•nee*
I'm busy.	**Llamkaywan kani.** *Yahm•kahy•wahn kah•nee*
I'm not interested.	**Mana munanichu.** *Mah•nah moo•nah•nee•choo*
Leave me alone.	**Anchhuy kaymanta.** *Ahn•chooy kahy•mahn•tah*
Stop bothering me!	**¡Mana toqllani!** *Mah•nah tohk•yah•nee*

Food & Drink

Eating Out

Can you recommend a good restaurant/bar? **¿Allin mikhuna wasi/bar yachankichu?** *Ah·yeen mee·koo·nah wah·see/bahr yah·chahn·kee·choo*

Is there a traditional/ an inexpensive restaurant nearby? **¿Huk barato mikhuna wasi kayllapi kanchu?** *Khuk bah·rah·too mee·koo·nah wah·see kahy·yah·pee kahn·choo*

A table for..., please. **Ama hina, huk hamp'ara ... runakunapaq.** *Ah·mah khee·nah, khook khahm·pah·rah ... roo·nah·koo·nah·pahk*

Can we sit...? **¿... tiyay atikuykuchu?** *... tee·yahy ah·tee·kooy·koo·choo*

  here/there **kaypi/chaypi** *kahy·pee/chahy·pee*

  outside **hawa** *khah·wah*

  in a non-smoking area **mana fumador kitipi** *mah·nah foo·mah·dohr kee·tee·pee*

I'm waiting for someone. **Huk runa suyani.** *Khook roo·nah soo·yah·nee*

Where are the toilets? **¿Maypi bañota kan?** *Mahy·pee bah·nyo·tah kahn*

The menu, please.	**Ama hina menuta.** *Ah·mah khee·nah meh·noo·tah*
What do you recommend?	**¿Ima nikunki?** *Ee·mah nee·koon·kee*
I'd like…	**… munani.** *… moo·nah·nee*
Some more…, please.	**Anchata.** *Ahn·chah·tah*
Enjoy your meal!	**¡Mikhunayki kusirikunki!** *Mee·koo·nahy·kee koo·see·ree·koon·kee*
The check [bill], please.	**Chaninta [factura], ama hinata.** *Chah·neen·tah [fahk·too·rah], ah·mah khee·nah·tah*
Is service included?	**¿Servicio yapasqanchu?** *Sehr·bee·thee·oh yah·pahs·kahn·choo*
Can I pay by credit card/have a receipt?	**¿Qullqiwan/manukuy tarjetawan payllay atikunichu?** *Kohl·keh·wahn/mah·noo·kooy tahr·khee·tah·w·ahn pahy·yahy ah·tee·koo·nee·choo*

YOU MAY SEE…

CHANIN PAGASQAN	cover charge
HUKLLA CHANIN	fixed price
MENU (KUNAN PUNCHAQPAQ)	menu (of the day)
SERVICIO (MANA) YAPASQAN	service (not) included
ESPECIALIDADKUNA	specials

Breakfast

tocino *toh·thee·noh*		bacon
t'anta *tahn·tah*		bread
mantequilla *mahn·teh·kee·yah*		butter
embutidokuna *ehm·boo·tee·do·koo·nah*		cold cuts
masara *mah·sah·rah*		cheese
...runtu *... roon·too*		...egg
seq'ayasqa runtu/runtu phasi		hard/soft-boiled
seh·kah·yahs·ka·roon·too/roon·too pah·see		
theqtiq runtu *tehk·teek roon·too*		fried
qaywisqa runtu *kahy·wees·kah roon·too*		scrambled
mermelada/jalea		jam/jelly
mehr·meh·lah·dah/khah·leh·ah		
omelet *oo·mee·leht*		omelet
t'antata ninapi paruy achiy		toast
tahn·tah·tah nee·nah·pee pah·rooy ah·cheey		
chorizo *choh·ree·thoo*		sausage
yogurt *yoh·goor*		yogurt

Appetizers

paté *pah·tee*		pâté
chawlla lawa *chahw·yah lah·wah*		fish soup
vegetales/tomate lawa		vegetable/tomato soup
veh·khe·tah·lehs/toh·mah·the lah·wah		
wallpa lawa *wahy·pah lah·wah*		chicken soup
leikkeleet *layk·ke·leht*		coldcuts
ensalada *ehn·sah·lah·dah*		salad

Meat

aycha *ahy·chah*		beef
wallpa *wahy·pah*		chicken

YOU MAY HEAR...

hanku aycha *kahn·koo ahy·chah*	rare
qhallwa aycha *kahy·wah ahy·chah*	medium
chayasqa aycha *chah·yahs·kah ahy·chah*	well-done

uwija *oo·wee·khah*	lamb
kuchi *koo·chee*	pork
mat'a *mah·tah*	steak
waka *wah·kah*	veal

Fish & Seafood

bacalau *bah·kah·laooh*	cod
chawlla croketa *chah·yah kroh·keh·tah*	fishcakes
arenque *Ah·rehn·keh*	herring
langosta *lahn·gohs·tah*	lobster
salmon *sahl·mohn*	salmon
yukra *yook·rah*	shrimp/prawn

Vegetables

purutu *Poo·roo·too*		beans
repollo *reh·poh·yoh*		cabbage
zanahoria *thah·nah·oh·ree·yah*		carrots
paku *pah·kooh*		mushroom
cebolla *theh·boh·yah*		onion
arwija *ahr·wee·khah*		peas
papa *pah·pah*		potato
tomate *Toh·mah·teh*		tomato

Sauces & Condiments

Salt	**Kachi** *Kah·chee*
Pepper	**Pimienta** *Pee·mee·yehn·tah*
Mustard	**Mostaza** *Mohs·tah·thah*
Ketchup	**Tomate llawqa** *Toh·mah·teh yahw·kah*

Fruit & Dessert

manzana *mahn·thah·nah*	apple
platanu *plah·tah·noo*	banana
limon *lee·mohn*	lemon
naranja *nah·rahn·khah*	orange
pera *peh·rah*	pear
fresas *freh·sahs*	strawberries
helado *eh·lah·doh*	ice cream
chocolate/vainilla *choh·coh·lah·teh/ bah·ee·nee·yah*	chocolate/vanilla
tarta/pastel *tahr·tah/pahs·tehl*	tart/cake
mousse *moos*	mousse
natilla/crema *nah·tee·yah/kreh·mah*	custard/cream

Drinks

The wine list/drink menu, please.	**Vino/upyana menu apamuriy.**	*Bee·noh/ oop·yah·nah meh·noo ah·pah·moo·reey*
What do you recommend?	**¿Ima nikunki?**	*Ee·mah nee·koon·kee*
I'd like a bottle/ glass of red/ white wine.	**Puka/yuraq vino botellapi/vasopi munani.**	*Poo·kah/yoo·rahk bee·noh boh·teh·yah·pee/ bah·soh·pee moo·nah·nee*
The house wine, please.	**Wasip vinon, ama hinata.**	*Wah·seep bee·nohn, ah·mah khee·nah·tah*
Another bottle/glass, please.	**Wak botellata/vasota apamuriy.**	*Wahk boh·teh·yah·tah/bah·soh·tah ah·pah·moo·reey*
I'd like a local beer.	**Cerveza llaqamanta munani.**	*Thehr·beh·sah yah·kah·mahn·tah moo·nah·nee*
Can I buy you a drink?	**¿Huk upyana rantiy atikunichu?**	*Khook oop·yah·nah rahn·teey ah·tee·koo·nee·choo*
Cheers!	**¡Anqoso!**	*Ahn·qoh·soh*
A coffee/tea, please.	**Huk café/te apamuriy.**	*Khuk kah·feh/teh ah·pah·moo·reey*
Black.	**Yuraq.**	*Yoo·rahk*
With...	**... kaqwan.**	*... kahk·wahn*
milk	**wilali**	*wee·lah·lee*
sugar	**misk'i**	*mees·kee*
artificial sweetener	**artificial misk'i**	*ahr·tee·fee·thee·ahl mees·kee*
A..., please.	**Huk... apamuriy.**	*Khook... Ah·pah·moo·reey*
juice	**jugu**	*khoo·goo*
soda [soft drink]	**soda [ch'akipa]**	*soh·dah [chah·kee·pah]*
(sparkling/still)	**(gaswan/mana gas) yaku**	*(gahs·wahn/mah·nah) yah·koo*
water		*yah·koo*

Leisure Time

Sightseeing

Where's the tourist information office?	**¿Maypi turística willaypa oficinan kan?** *Mahy·pee too·rees·tee·kah wee·yahy·pah oh·fee·thee·nahn kahn*
What are the main sights?	**¿Ima mapa turistico kitita kanku?** *Ee·mah mah·pah too·rees·tee·koh kee·tee·tah kahn·koo*
Do you offer tours in English?	**¿Watukuykuna Inglespi qunki?** *Wah·too·kooy·koo·nah Een·glehs·pee koon·kee*
Can I have a map/guide?	**¿Huk mapa/guia tiyay atikuni?** *Khook mah·pah/gee·ah tee·yahy ah·tee·koo·nee*

Shopping

Where's the market/mall?	**¿Maypi qatu/rantiy kanchu?** *Mahy·pee kah·too/rahn·teey kahn·choo*
I'm just looking.	**Maskachkanilla.** *Mahs·kahch·kahn·nee·yah*

YOU MAY SEE...

KICHAY/WICHQ'AY	open/closed
HAYKUNA/LLUQSINA	entrance/exit

Can you help me?	**¿Yanapaway atikunki?** *Yah-nah-pah-wahy ah-tee-koon-kee*	
I'm being helped.	**Yanapakusqa kachkani.** *Yah-nah-pah-koos-kah kahch-kah-nee*	
How much?	**¿Machka chaniyuq?** *Mahch-kah chah-nee-yohk*	
That one, please.	**Kay huklla, ama hinata.** *K ahy khook-yah ama khee-nah-tah*	
I'd like…	**… munani.** *… moo-nah-nee*	
That's all.	**Llapallan.** *Yah-pah-yahn*	
Where can I pay?	**¿Maypi payllay atikuni?** *Mahy-pee pahy-yahy ah-tee-koo-nee*	
I'll pay in cash/ by credit card.	**Qullqiwan/manukuy tarjetawan payllani.** *Kohl-keh-wahn/mah-noo-kooy tahr-kheh-tah-wahn pahy-yah-nee*	
A receipt, please.	**Factura, ama hinata.** *Fahk-too-rah ah-mah khee-nah-tah*	

Sport & Leisure

When's the game?	**¿Maypi pukllayta kanchu?** *Mahy-pee pook-yahy-tah kahn-choo*	
Where's…?	**¿Maypi…kanchu?** *Mahy-pee … kahn-choo*	
the beach	**qochapata** *koh-chah-pah-tah*	
the park	**parkita** *phar-kee-tah*	
the pool	**piscinata** *pees-thee-nah-ta*	
Is it safe to swim here?	**¿Kaypi chiqa wayt'ay kanchu?** *Kahy-pee cheh-kah wahy-tahy kahn-choo*	
Can I hire clubs?	**¿Clubkuna mink'ay atikunichu?** *Cloob-koo-nah meen-kahy ah-tee-koo-nee-choo*	
How much per hour/ day?	**¿Machka chaniyuq sapa pachata/punchawta?** *Mahch-kah chah-nee-yohk sah-pa pah-chah-tah/poon-chaoo-tah*	

How far is it to…?	**¿Imata karumanta … kaqman kanchu?** *Eeh·mah·tah kah·roo·man·tah kahk·mahn kahn·choo*
Show me on the map, please.	**Ama hina mapapi qawapaway.** *Ah·mah khee·nah mah·pah·pee qah·wah·pah·way*

Going Out

What's there to do at night?	**¿Imataq tutarayku ruwayta kanchu?** *Eeh·mah·tahk too·tah·ray·koo roo·wahy·tah kahn·choo*
Do you have a program of events?	**¿Huk intiwatana raymipi tiyankichu?** *Hook een·tee·wah·tah·nah rahy·mee·pee tee·yan·kee·choo*
What's playing tonight?	**¿Ima kay tuta purichkanchu?** *Ee·mah kahy too·tah poo·reech·kahn·choo*
Where's…?	**¿Maypi … kanchu?** *Mahy·pee kahn·choo*
the downtown area	**chawpi llaqtamanta** *chaoo·pee yahk·tah·mahn·tah*
the bar	**barta** *bahr·tah*
the dance club	**club takiypaq** *cloob tah·keey·pahk*
Is this area at night?	**¿Kay kiti chiqa tutapi kanchu?** *Kahy kee·tee cheh·kah too·tah·pee kahn·choo*

Baby Essentials

Do you have…?	**¿… tiyankichu?** … *tee·yahn·kee·choo*
a baby bottle	**huk biberonta** *khook bee·beh·rohn·tah*
baby food	**mikhuna wawapaq** *meek·koo·nah wah·wah·pahk*
baby wipes	**toallakuna wawapaq** *toh·ah·yah·kooh·nah wah·wah·pahk*
a car seat	**huk tiyana autopaq** *khook tee·yah·nah aw·toh·pahk*
a children's menu/ portion	**huk menu/porción wawapaq** *Khuk mee·noo/ pohr·thee·yohn wah·wah·pahk*
a child's seat/ highchair	**huk tiyana/huchuy tiyana wawapaq** *khook tee·yah·nah/khoo·chooy tee·yah·nah wah·wah·pahk*
a crib/cot	**huk tankana** *khook tahn·kah·nah*
diapers [nappies]	**pañalkuna** *pah·nyahl·koo·nah*
formula	**formula** *foor·moo·lah*
a pacifier [dummy]	**huk chupete** *khook choo·peh·teh*
a playpen	**huk kancha wawapaq** *kook kahn·chah wah·wah·pahk*
a stroller [pushchair]	**huk auto wawapaq** *kook aw·too wah·wah·pahk*
Can I breastfeed the baby here?	**¿Kaypi waway ñuñuyta atikunichu?** *Kahy·pee wah·wahy nyoo·nyooy·tah ah·tee·koo·nee·choo*

| Where can I breastfeed/change the baby? | **¿Maypi waway ñuñuy/tikray atikunichu?** *Mahy•pee wah•wahy nyoo•nyooy/teek•rahy ah•tee•koo•nee•choo* |

For Eating Out, see page 206

Disabled Travelers

Is there…?	**¿Kaypi…kanchu?** *Kahy•pee … kahn•choo*
access for the disabled	**minusválidos yaykuna** *mee•noos•vah•lee•dohs yahy•koo•nah*
a wheelchair ramp	**rampa silla de ruedas nisqapaq** *rahm•pah see•yah deh rweh•dahs nees•kah•pahk*
a disabled-accessible toilet	**huk baño minusvalidospaq** *khook bah•nyoh mee•noos•vah•lee•dohs•pahk*
I need…	**… munani.** *… moo•nah•nee*
assistance	**Yanapakuyta** *Yah•nah•pah•kooy•tah*
an elevator [a lift]	**Huk ascensor** *Khook ah•thehn•sohr*
a ground-floor room	**Huk habitación uraypi panpa** *Khook ah•bee•tah•theeyohn ooh•rahy•pee phan•pah*
Please speak louder.	**Sinchi parlariy.** *Seen•chee pahr•lah•reey*

Health & Emergencies

Emergencies

Help!	**¡Yanapakuy!**	*Yah•nah•pah•kooy*
Go away!	**¡Anchhuy kaymanta!**	*Ahn•chooy kahy•mahn•tah*
Stop, thief!	**¡Mana, suwaq!**	*Mah•nah soo•wahk*
Get a doctor!	**¡Huk hampiq tariy!**	*Khook hahm•peek tah•reey*
Fire!	**¡Nana!**	*Nah•nah*
I'm lost.	**Chinkaykachani.**	*Cheen•kahy•kah•chah•nee*

YOU MAY HEAR...

Kay formulario qillqay.
Kahy foor•moo•lah•reeyoo kehy•kahy

Fill out this form.

ID nisqayki, quriy. *doh•koo•mehn•toh deh ee•dehn•tee•dahd nees•kahy•kee •koo•reey*

Your ID, please.

¿Hayk'aq/Maypi karunqa? *Khay•kahk/ May•pee kah•roon•kha*

When/Where did it happen?

¿Ima pay kan? *Eeh•mah pahy kahn*

What does he/she look like?

Can you help me?	**¿Yanapaway atikunkichu?** *Yah-nah-pah-wahy ah-tee-koon-kee-choo*
Call the police!	**¡Policiaman qayay!** *poh-leh-tee-ah-mahn kha-yahy*
Where's the police station?	**¿Maypi policia estacionta kanchu?** *Mahy-pee poh-lee-thee-ah ehs-tah-theeyohn-tah kahn-choo*
My child is missing.	**Waway chinkaykachan.** *Wah-wahy cheen-kahy-chahn*

Health

I'm sick.	**Unquq kani.** *Oon-kook kah-nee*
I need an English-speaking doctor.	**Huk hampiq Ingles simipi parlayta munani.** *Khook hahm-peek Een-glehs see-mee-pee pahr-lahy-tah moo-nah-nee*
It hurts here.	**Kaypi nanan.** *Kahy-pee nahn-nahn*
Where's the pharmacy?	**¿Maypi farmaciata kanchu?** *Mahy-pee fahr-mah-thee-yah-tah kahn-choo*
I'm (...months) pregnant.	**Wiksayuq (... killawan) kani.** *Week-sah-yohk (... kee-yah-wahn) kah-nee*
I'm on...	**... kaqpi kani.** *... kahk-pee kah-nee*
I'm allergic to antibiotics/penicillin.	**Alergia ... kani antibioticokunata/penicilinata.** *Ah-lehr-kee-ah ... kah-nee ahn-tee-beeyoh-tee-kohs-ko o-nah-tah peh-nee-thee-lee-nah-tah*

Check the local emergency numbers in your locality upon arrival as these will vary from region to region.

Dictionary

A

a huk *khook*

acetaminophen [paracetamol] acetaminofeno [paracetamol] *ah·theh·tah·mee·noh·feh noo [pah·rah·thee·tah·mohl]*

adaptor uyachaq *ooh·yah·chahk*

aid worker yanapaq *yah·nah·pahk*

and chaymanta *chaeeh·mahn·tah*

antiseptic cream crema antiseptica *kreh·mah ahn·tee·sehp·tee·kah*

aspirin aspirina *ahs·pee·ree·nah*

B

baby wawa *ooh·ah·ooh·ah*

a backpack huk mochila *khook moh·chee·lah*

bad mana allin *mah·nah ah·yeen*

bag bolso *bool·soo*

Band-Aid [plasters] Curita [yesokuna] *Koo·ree·tah [yeh·soh·koo·nah]*

bandages vendakuna *ven·dah·koo·nah*

battleground awqatinku kiti *ahw·kah·teen·kooh kee·tee*

bee lachiwa *lah·chee·wah*

beige beige *beh·yees*

bikini bikini *bee·kee·nee*

bird pisqu *pehs·koh*

black yana *yah·nah*

bland (food) chuma (mikhuna) *choo·mah (mee·koo·nah)*

blue anqas *ahn·kahs*

bottle opener botella kichaq *boh·teh·yah kee·chahk*

bowl urpu *oor·poo*

boy wayna *wahy·nah*

boyfriend munakuq *moo·nah·kook*

bra sujetador *soo·kheh·tah·dohr*
brown café *kah·feh*

C

camera camara *kah·mah·rah*
can opener lata kichaq *lah·tah kee·chahk*
cat misi *mee·see*
castle castillo *kahs·tee·yoh*
charger cargador *kahr·gah·dohr*
cigarettes cigarrillokuna *thee·gah·ree·yoh·koo·nah*
cold ch'iri *chee·ree*
comb (n) ñaqch'a *nyakh·chah*
computer computadora *cohm·poo·tah·doo·rah*
condoms preservativos nisqa *preh·sehr·bah·tee·bohs nees·kah*
contact lens solution solución lentes contactopaq *soh·loo·theeyohn lehn·tehs kohn·tahk·toh·pahk*
corkscrew sacacorchokuna *sah·kah·kohr·chohs·koo·nah*
cup taza *tah·thah*

D

dangerous phiru *peeh·rooh*
deodorant desodorante *deh·soh·doh·rahn·teh*
diabetic diabetico *dee·ah·beh·tee·koh*
dog alqu *ahl·koo*
doll muñeca *moo·nyeh·kah*

F

fly n phaway *phah·wahy*
fork tenedor *teh·neh·dohr*

G

girl sipas *see·pahs*
girlfriend munakuq *moo·nah·kook*

glass vaso *bah•soh*
good allin *ah•yeen*
gray oqe *oh•keh*
great hatun *khah•toon*
green q'omer *koh•mehr*

H

a hairbrush huk ñaqch'a chukchapaq *khook nyahk•chah chook•chah•pahk*
hairspray laka chukchapaq *lah•kah chook•chah•pahk*
horse cawallu *kah•ooah•yooh*
hot q'oñi *khoh•nyee*
husband qusa *koo•sah*

I

ibuprofen ibuprofeno *ee•boo•proh•feh•noh*
ice chullunku *choo•yoon•koo*
icy qasasqa *kah•sahs•kah*
injection inyeccion *een•yeh•kee•ohn*
I'd like… … munani.… *moo•nah•nee*
insect repellent repelente insectospaq *reh•peh•lehn•tee een•sehk•tohs•phak*

J

jeans vaqueros *bah•keh•rohs*

K

(steak) knife (mat'a) kuchuna *(mah•tah) koo•choo•nah*

L

lactose intolerant mana chakikuy lactosa *mah•nah chah•kee•kooy lahk•toh•sah*
large suni *soo•nee*
lighter rawrachiq *raoh•rah•cheek*
lion leon *leh•ohn*

lotion [moisturizing cream] locion [crema hidratante] *loh·theeon [creh·mah ee·drah·tahn·tee]*

love munasqa *moo·nahs·kah*

M

matches cerillas *theh·ree·yahs*

medium chawpi *chaoo·pee*

monkey mono *moo·noo*

museum museo *moo·seh·oh*

my ...y ... *ee*

N

a nail file huk lima sillukunapaq *khook leeh·mah see·yoo·koo·na·phak*

napkin servilleta *sehr·bee·yeh·tah*

nurse enfermerakuna *ehn·fehr·meh·rah*

O

or utaq *oo·thak*

orange q'illu puka *keh·yoo poo·kah*

P

park parki *pahr·kee*

partner masi *mah·see*

pen qillqana *kehy·kah·na*

pink yanqa puka *yahn·kah poo·kah*

plate oqe *oh·keh*

purple willapi *wee·yha·pee*

pyjamas pijamakuna *pee·khah·mah·koo·nah*

R

rain para *pah·rah*

a raincoat huk impermeable *khook eem·pehr·meh·ah·bleh*

a (disposable) razor huk (desechable) makina afeitarpaq *khuk (deh•seh•chah•bleh) mah•kee•nah ah•fehy•tahr•pahk*
razor blades hojas razurarpaq *oh•kahs rah•thoo•rahr•pahk*
red puka *poo•kha*

S

safari safari *sah•phah•ree*
salty kachi *kah•chee*
a sauna huk sauna *khook sawoo•nah*
sandals sandaliakuna *sahn•dah•leeyahs koo•nah*
sanitary napkins [pads] servilleta sanitariakuna
(almohadillakuna) *sehr•bee•yeh•tah sah•nee•tah•reeah•koo•nah*
(*ahl•moo•hah•dee•yah•koo•nah*)
scissors k'utuchina *koo•tooh•chee•nah*
shampoo/conditioner shampoo/suavizante *chahm•poo/swah•bee•thahn•teh*
shoes papatos *pah•pah•toos*
small huchuy *khoo•chooy*
snake katari *kah•tah•ree*
sneakers paptukuna pukllaypaq *pahp•too•koo•nah pook•yay•pahk*
snow rit'i *ree•tee*
soap jabon *khah•bohn*
socks mediakuna *meh•diah•koo•nah*
spicy uchu *oo•choo*
spider apasanka *ah•pah•sahn•kah*
spoon cuchara *koo•chah•rah*
a sweater huk chompa *khook chohm•pah*
stamp(s) sello(kuna) *seh•yoh (koo•nah)*
suitcase maleta *mah•leh•tah*
sun inti *een•tee*
sunglasses lentes intipaq *lehn•tehs een•tee•pahk*
sunscreen protector intipaq *proh•tehk•tohr een•tee•pahk*
a sweatshirt huk sudadera *khook soo•dah•deh•rah*

a swimsuit huk traje bañopaq *hook trah·kheh bah·nyoh·pahk*

T

a T-shirt huk camiseta *khook kah·mee·seh·tah*
tampons tamponkuna *tahm·pohn·koo·nah*
terrible adj terrible *teh·reeh·bleh*
tie corbata *kohr·bah·tah*
tissues pañuelokuna *pah·nyweh·loh·koo·nah*
toilet paper papel higienico *pah·pehl ee·kheeyeh·nee·koh*
toothbrush cepillo karukunapaq *theh·pee·yoh kah·roo·koo·nah·pahk*
toothpaste pasta karukunapaq *pahs·tah kah·roo·koo·nah·pahk*
tough (meat) kuku (aycha) *koo·koo (ah·eeh·chah)*
toy juguete *khoo·geh·teh*

U

underwear interiorpaq p'acha *een·teh·reeyohr·pahk phah·chah*

V

vegetarian vegetarian *beh·kheh·tah·reeyah·noo*
vegan vegano *beh·gah·noo*

W

white yuraq *yooh·rahk*
with ...wan *...wahn*
wife warmi *wahr·mee*
without manaña *mah·nah·ñah*

Y

yellow q'illu *kheh·yoo*
your qam *kahm*

Z

zoo zoologico *thoh·oh·loh·khee·koh*